HARNESSING THE ECONOMIC POTENTIAL OF INDIA'S CITIES

JUNE 2024

ASIAN DEVELOPMENT BANK

 Creative Commons Attribution 3.0 IGO license (CC BY 3.0 IGO)

© 2024 Asian Development Bank
6 ADB Avenue, Mandaluyong City, 1550 Metro Manila, Philippines
Tel +63 2 8632 4444; Fax +63 2 8636 2444
www.adb.org

Some rights reserved. Published in 2024.

ISBN 978-92-9270-769-9 (print); 978-92-9270-770-5 (PDF); 978-92-9270-771-2 (ebook)
Publication Stock No. TCS240320-2
DOI: http://dx.doi.org/10.22617/TCS240320-2

The views expressed in this publication are those of the authors and do not necessarily reflect the views and policies of the Asian Development Bank (ADB) or its Board of Governors or the governments they represent.

ADB does not guarantee the accuracy of the data included in this publication and accepts no responsibility for any consequence of their use. The mention of specific companies or products of manufacturers does not imply that they are endorsed or recommended by ADB in preference to others of a similar nature that are not mentioned.

By making any designation of or reference to a particular territory or geographic area in this document, ADB does not intend to make any judgments as to the legal or other status of any territory or area.

This publication is available under the Creative Commons Attribution 3.0 IGO license (CC BY 3.0 IGO) https://creativecommons.org/licenses/by/3.0/igo/. By using the content of this publication, you agree to be bound by the terms of this license. For attribution, translations, adaptations, and permissions, please read the provisions and terms of use at https://www.adb.org/terms-use#openaccess.

This CC license does not apply to non-ADB copyright materials in this publication. If the material is attributed to another source, please contact the copyright owner or publisher of that source for permission to reproduce it. ADB cannot be held liable for any claims that arise as a result of your use of the material.

Please contact pubsmarketing@adb.org if you have questions or comments with respect to content, or if you wish to obtain copyright permission for your intended use that does not fall within these terms, or for permission to use the ADB logo.

Corrigenda to ADB publications may be found at http://www.adb.org/publications/corrigenda.

Notes:
In this publication, "$" refers to United States dollars and "₹" refers to Indian rupees.
ADB recognizes "China" as the People's Republic of China, "Russia" as the Russian Federation, and "Korean" as referring to the Republic of Korea.

Cover design by Joe Mark Ganaban.

Contents

Tables, Figures, and Boxes v
Acknowledgments vii
Abbreviations viii
Executive Summary ix

Chapter 1: **Introduction** 1
    Background 1
    Scope of the Study 8
    Approach of the Study 11

Chapter 2: **Shortlisting Cities for Study** 15
    Concept of Natural Cities Based on Nighttime Lights 15
    Selection of Cities 18

Chapter 3: **City Profiles—Economic Activity and Spatial Growth** 22
    Dewas 22
    Gangtok 24
    Guwahati 25
    Hisar 27
    Indore 28
    Machilipatnam 30
    Nalgonda 32
    Navsari 33
    Sonipat 34
    Vadodara 36
    Vijayawada 37
    Warangal 39
    Summary 40

Chapter 4: **Stakeholder Consultations to Identify Growth Bottlenecks** 42

Chapter 5: **Key Bottlenecks Constraining the Potential of Cities** 47
    Lack of Common Economic Vision 47
    Challenges Related to Land 49
    Lack of Integrated Approach to Master Planning 50
    Inadequate Institutional Frameworks and Capacity Constraints 53
    Business-Related Policies and Regulatory Constraints 54

Chapter 6:	**Recommendations**	58
	An Economic Vision for the City	58
	Land Supply for Enabling Development	65
	Integrated Master Planning	70
	Institutional Integration and Capacity Building in Development and Planning	77
	Policies and Regulations Governing Business Activity in Cities	79
Chapter 7:	**Conclusions**	85

Tables, Figures, and Boxes

Tables

1.1	Addressing Bottlenecks	12
2.1	Economic Structure of Indore Natural City Versus Indore Urban Agglomeration	17
2.2	The Twelve Selected Cities	18
2.3	Economic Potential Index Components	19
2.4	Thresholds for Economic Potential Index Ratings	19
2.5	Selected Cities	20
4.1	Key Structured Interview Themes for Government Stakeholders	44
4.2	Key Structured Interview Themes for Private Sector Stakeholders	45
5.1	Incentives in India for Manufacturing	55
6.1	Action Areas for Removing Bottlenecks to City Economic Growth	58
6.2	Land-Use Structure for Developable Area in Urban Centers	71
6.3	Examples of Policies and Regulations at the City Level	80

Figures

1.1	Generic Landscape of Urban Institutions' and Actors' Responsibilities in Indian Cities	9
1.2	Institutional Structure for Planning and Developing an Industrial Park	10
1.3	Study Approach	11
2.1	Illustration of a Natural City—Indore, Madhya Pradesh	16
3.1	Spatial Development of Dewas Natural City, 2000 and 2016	23
3.2	Gangtok Administrative City	24
3.3	Spatial Development of Guwahati Natural City, 2000 and 2016	26
3.4	Spatial Development of Hisar Natural City, 2000 and 2016	28
3.5	Spatial Development of Indore Natural City, 2000 and 2016	29
3.6	Spatial Development of Machilipatnam Natural City, 2000 and 2016	31
3.7	Spatial Development of Nalgonda Natural City, 2000 and 2016	32
3.8	Spatial Development of Navsari Natural City, 2000 and 2016	34
3.9	Spatial Snapshot of Sonipat Administrative City	35
3.10	Spatial Development of Vadodara Natural City, 2000 and 2016	37
3.11	Spatial Development of Vijayawada Natural City, 2000 and 2016	38
3.12	Spatial Development of Warangal Natural City, 2000 and 2016	40
4.1	Stakeholders Involved	43
5.1	Key Bottlenecks that Constrain Cities from Realizing their Economic Potential	48
6.1	A Possible Governance Model for a City Economic Council	65

Boxes

1.1 What Accounts for Agglomeration Economies? 2
1.2 Managing the Benefits and Costs of Agglomeration 4
1.3 India's Urban System 5
1.4 Policies for Making Cities more Livable 7
5.1 Setting Up a Hotel in a City 56
6.1 Local Economic Development Strategy for Cities 59
6.2 Six Cities' Growth Visions, Actions, and Outcomes..60
6.3 Interlinking Spatial Planning with Economic Planning—The South African Case..............73
6.4 Capital Investment Planning—City of Nis in Serbia...73
6.5 Developing Technopoles in India..76
6.6 Singapore Cooperation Enterprise 79

Acknowledgments

This report was prepared in response to a request by NITI Aayog to examine how India's cities can meet their full economic potential and thereby support India's states and union territories in achieving broad-based urban development. The report was supported by an Asian Development Bank (ADB) technical assistance project, TA 9508: Country Diagnostic Studies in Selected Developing Member Countries (Subproject 4).

The report was prepared by a team from ADB and PricewaterhouseCoopers Pvt. Ltd. and with contributions from Anshika Gupta, specialist, Urban Development, NITI Aayog. The ADB Team was led by Rana Hasan and Lei Lei Song and included Yi Jiang; Maria Rowena M. Cham; Milan Thomas; Iva Sebastian-Samaniego; Glenita Amoranto; Benedict M. Evangelista, Jr. (ADB consultant); and Marjorie Villanueva Remolador (ADB consultant). Madhusree Dasgupta, Chinmaya Goyal, Naimat Chopra (ADB consultant) and Kriti Jain (ADB consultant) reviewed the report.

The PricewaterhouseCoopers Team and its associates comprised Mohammad Athar, who conceptualized the framework used in Chapters 5 and 6; Sujay Shetty; Sreedhar Pothukuchi; Udit Sharma; Sanskar Mehta; Madhu Bala CV; Bhanu Nelavalli; Seetha Raghupathy from Seagull Studio; and Neha Sami and Shriya Anand from the India Institute of Human Settlements.

The report benefited from a team of advisors comprising Gyanendra Badgaiyan, resident senior fellow, Infrastructure Development Finance Company Institute; V Srinivas Chary, director, Centre for Urban Governance, Environment, Energy and Infrastructure Development, Administrative Staff College of India; and Partha Mukhopadhyay, senior faculty, Centre for Policy Research.

The report was edited by Jill Gale de Villa. Joe Mark Ganaban did the graphic design, layout, and typesetting. Rajeev Sundaram and Gee Ann Carol Burac provided administrative support.

Abbreviations

AC	—	administrative city
CEC	—	city economic council
GDP	—	gross domestic product
GIS	—	geographic information system
ha	—	hectare
ID	—	identification
IT	—	information technology
km^2	—	square kilometer
MSMEs	—	micro, small, and medium-sized enterprises
MTDCC	—	Magarpatta Township Development and Construction Company
NC	—	natural city
NICDC	—	National Industrial Corridor Development Corporation
SEZ	—	special economic zone
SIR	—	special investment region
SPV	—	special purpose vehicle
TPS	—	town planning scheme
UA	—	urban agglomeration
ULB	—	urban local body

Executive Summary

Background of the Study

Global evidence, based on both historical and recent experience, demonstrates the close association of urbanization with an increase in per capita incomes. As countries develop, economic activity shifts from agriculture to manufacturing and services. Locationally, this shift is accompanied by the growth of urban centers, which in turn is driven by the ability of cities and their surrounding areas to efficiently produce manufactured goods and services, create jobs, and catalyze innovation. By enabling firms and workers to interact closely, cities generate increased productivity through several channels, collectively known as "agglomeration economies."

Given the importance of the urbanization–economic growth relationship, the urbanization process unfolding in India holds much promise for the country's economic aspirations. While in 2011 just 31.1% of India's population was urban (377 million people), projections indicate that the share will increase to 50% by the middle of the century, adding about 400 million people to India's cities. For India to achieve its goal of becoming a high-income economy by 2047, it is crucial that its cities fulfill their potential as engines of economic growth.

Harnessing the full economic potential of India's cities requires recognizing the need for action on two fronts. First, the forces of agglomeration should be carefully managed as, beyond a tipping point, productivity gains due to colocation of workers and industries may be limited by congestion's negative impact on productivity. Second, cities are connected to one another and to the rural hinterland; thus, a polycentric growth model that enables seamless flows of goods, services, and people across large, medium, and small cities is important to ensure comprehensive economic growth. Consequently, the focus should not only be on nurturing megacities, but equally on smaller cities as centers of economic growth.

This study focuses on developing a framework that states and their cities can use to foster greater economic growth and job creation. Two key objectives of the study are (i) identifying bottlenecks that constrain Indian cities from fully realizing their potential as engines of growth; and (ii) developing implementable solutions to the bottlenecks, including workable mechanisms for coordinating spatial and economic planning.

To achieve the objectives, the study took the following steps.

Step 1: Shortlisting Cities and Developing City Profiles

Twelve cities from seven states were selected as case studies for analyzing bottlenecks to economic growth and proposing frameworks for synchronizing economic and spatial planning. A top-down three-tier approach (state, district, and city) was used to arrive at a shortlist of the 12 cities. In the first step, five states were identified based on regional diversity and indicators of urban and economic development—Gujarat, Haryana, Madhya Pradesh, Sikkim, and Telangana. Two states were eventually added to this list: Assam, the largest urban area in the northeastern region; and Andhra Pradesh, which is traversed by the East Coast Economic Corridor and where maximizing synergies between industry and urbanization are a key planning feature.

Next, only cities in districts with reasonably high scores on an index of district-level economic potential were identified as candidates for the study. This was done to ensure that key enablers for establishing modern businesses were available in case study cities and their surrounding areas. Key enablers included the distance of a district's headquarters from major cities in India and the working age population's secondary school completion rates. Finally, to arrive at a shortlist of 1–2 cities per state, several steps were taken, including limiting attention to cities with populations between 100,000 and 3 million, dropping cities that were immediate neighbors of mega cities, and prioritizing cities that specialized in manufacturing or modern business services.

Cities were also defined in terms of the concept of a "natural city." Such cities are defined using nighttime lights data from satellite images and cover statutory towns with a population greater than 100,000 as of the year 2000, along with neighboring towns and villages that are contiguously illuminated.

Finally, a brief profile was developed for each shortlisted city, describing its economic potential (such as key growth and investment sectors, composition of output, and employment activities), and the trajectory of spatial growth of economic activity. This assessment was carried out based on data available from databases such as the Economic Census 2013, states' economic surveys, nighttime lights data, and the Asian Development Bank's natural city data of 2000–2016.

Step 2: Consulting Stakeholders

More than 130 stakeholder consultations were carried out to understand and identify bottlenecks constraining the economic potential of cities.

Discussions with government stakeholders at all levels (local, state, and central) were held to understand the broader economic–spatial relations, the urban and peri-urban dynamics, and the granular set of factors driving economic growth in the states and cities examined.

Discussions with private sector actors were held to better understand the practical challenges and benefits of doing business in the region—interviewees included investors; developers; industry associations; and small, medium, and large companies and entrepreneurs.

Step 3: Assessing Bottlenecks

Stakeholder interactions revealed that despite the diversity of the cities studied, they had in common many factors holding them back from realizing their economic potential. The factors can be grouped in terms of five broad bottlenecks: (i) lack of common economic vision, (ii) challenges related to land supply, (iii) unintegrated planning of urban and industrial infrastructure, (iv) inadequate institutional framework and capacity, and (v) business-related policy and regulatory constraints.

Economic vision. Without an economic vision to guide decision making at the level of a city (taken here to include neighboring areas whose economies are closely intertwined), urban areas have grown without leaving sufficient space for rights-of-ways and provision of basic infrastructure that is essential for economic dynamism. In fact, the absence of a city-level economic vision appears to be closely connected to several other bottlenecks identified in the stakeholder consultations. For example, without an economic vision, city master planning exercises tend to focus entirely on land-use and spatial and zoning regulations and do not inform infrastructure investment plans needed to realize economic goals. Similarly, the absence of a well-articulated economic vision for the city implies that economic visioning exercises carried out at the state level by state industry and planning departments lack an explicit spatial dimension that can serve as an anchor for agencies focusing on urban development.

Land. As India's economy and population continue to grow, serviced urban land is becoming increasingly scarce and competing claims are made on a finite supply. In addition, land acquisition on the urban periphery also triggers an economic transition from an agrarian-based economy to one that is increasingly dominated by secondary or tertiary industries. If this happens in an unplanned way, such areas tend to develop as an unmanageable sprawl devoid of basic facilities.

Integrated master planning. Cities' master plans largely do not articulate development goals based on which actual investments and mixed-use developments can be planned and implemented. Thus, as cities evolve and expand, their master plans have remained mainly static and account inadequately for future demands for land use and allocations. This has led to inadequate planning of growth-enabling infrastructure.

Institutional framework and capacity. Natural cities often cover multiple administrative units, sometimes spanning more than one district and multiple towns and many villages. Planning for economic development at this geographic scale clearly calls for cross-jurisdiction governance to effectively manage cities and their periphery. However, such governance is absent across the study cities.

Further, city governments play a limited role in influencing and coordinating the work of different agencies at the local level and even less in guiding economic development, despite the devolution of power to urban local bodies (ULBs) mandated by the 74th Constitutional Amendment. Instead, ULBs in India primarily deal with providing basic urban services and depend heavily on the state and central governments to finance infrastructure development and provide key social amenities. They do not have the functions or responsibilities to attract investments, nor a mandate to provide the ancillary and supporting infrastructure for fostering local economic development. This has limited the capacity and ability of India's cities to actively direct and manage economic transformation, in sharp contrast to cities in a wide range of middle- and high-income countries, which tend to have much more say in functions related to economic development.

Business-related policy and regulation. The policy and regulatory framework that firms face at any given location in India is influenced primarily by the central and relevant state governments. ULBs have played a limited role in contributing to the design of these incentives and programs because responsibility for local economic development largely does not rest with ULBs. However, one way city-level governments or ULBs can influence the business environment is by setting development norms to which businesses must adhere, thereby influencing the ease of starting and operating businesses, especially in various services subsectors. Strategies to make their city an attractive location for businesses seem to be largely missing. Addressing these issues is important to enhance the ease of doing business in Indian cities.

The foregoing five bottlenecks are likely to apply to most cities in India. However, some problem areas tend to be specific to certain cities. For example, locational disadvantages are more relevant for cities in hilly and mountainous areas or where climate patterns combine with topography to make a city prone to floods or droughts. Similarly, the lack of a historical industrial base—due to distance from major historical transport networks and urban centers of the country—can act as a drag on economic growth, a situation that affects some cities to a greater extent than other cities.

Step 4: Suggesting Solutions

To address the bottlenecks requires an integrated approach to urban and economic planning. The five themes and goals around which such an approach can be designed and implemented, as well as the actions that hold promise in achieving the goals, are listed as follows. Implementing many of the actions is likely to entail some challenges. However, the economic payoff is likely to be immense and go a long way in enabling India to meet its aspiration of becoming a high-income economy by 2047.

To develop an economic vision

- institute a city economic council with a governance structure that is tailored to state and city characteristics;
- ensure that the council is supported by representatives from the private sector and experts in economic and urban development;
- ensure that the economic vision for the city has a regional spatial strategy aligned with it;
- create city partnerships for thematic development opportunities and implementation; and
- develop a graded and certified program for enhancing the capacity of key stakeholders involved in planning and implementing the economic vision.

To supply land needed for development

- modernize and digitize the land records systems and make them interoperable across departments;

- integrate institutions of revenue, registration, and survey at the state level to harmonize land records data;

- establish integrated digital technology platforms to improve the efficiency of land transactions; and

- explore participatory land assembly mechanisms.

To achieve integrated master planning aligned with economic goals

- adopt a regional approach to planning by (i) demarcating the larger urban region, and (ii) planning the city and commuting area together;

- ensure that the master plan allows for actionable short-term milestones guided by a long-term strategic vision;

- develop a capital investment plan to identify projects that are aligned with the city's economic vision, economically sound, and self-sustaining;

- explore developing a cluster-based planning mechanism based on local labor competencies, material resources, and connectivity considerations;

- create provisions that facilitate change in land-use definitions and regulations at predefined time periods and with a detailed understanding of the range and scope of contemporary industries;

- coordinate among agencies and align details in technical documents and implementation guidelines to integrate the economic vision with the master plan;

- formulate an interdepartmental team led by appropriate officials to check the progress and outcomes of projects; and

- prepare project action plans for key proposals, specifying milestones, relevant agencies, and their collaboration mechanisms.

To strengthen institutional frameworks and build capacity

- create mechanisms enabling ULBs and relevant urban departments to participate in economic planning and visioning processes;

- engage public and private stakeholders in integrated approaches that bring together urban planning and economic visioning processes across levels and sectors;

- build multiple timeframes into economic strategies (5-, 10-, and 20-year periods), and incorporate incentives for public agencies to identify and respond to the needs of local populations and communities;

- review the functions that local and state-level agencies perform and rationalize their roles and responsibilities to minimize overlaps and improve clarity and accountability;

- reduce overlapping roles and responsibilities by developing structures to streamline functions across levels and improve communication and coordination;

- invest directly in expanding ULB staff to keep up with the demands of urban expansion; and

- expand support and training programs focusing on building capacity and regularly upgrading knowledge and skills.

To create a policy and regulatory environment conducive to business activity

- develop city-specific marketing programs (aligned with the city's vision) to support investments in the city;

- explore setting up an investment promotion agency for cities;

- create city-level single window facilities for service industries based within city limits (such as hospitality, healthcare, commercial developments, and education);

- enable, more generally, automated/digital approval mechanisms that are recognized by all state and ULB departments, and mandate timebound services provision for businesses in the city; and

- empower local bodies in and for industrial areas not under ULBs to better coordinate the functions and activities of industry and urban development departments.

Chapter 1

Introduction

Background

The global evidence indicates that urbanization is closely associated with increases in per capita incomes. One of the most widely recognized facts in economic development is that urbanization strongly correlates with income (for example, Henderson 2010). Examining urbanization rates and real gross domestic product (GDP) per capita for the world as a whole and developing Asia for each decade since 1970, a 1 percentage point increase in urbanization is associated with 3%–5% higher real GDP per capita (ADB 2019). Further, countries undergoing robust economic growth experience rapid urbanization at the same time. Examining the relationship between the growth rate of real GDP per capita and change in urbanization rate at 5-year intervals from 1970 and 2015 indicates that a 1 percentage point increase in the urbanization rate is associated with an estimated 3.2% higher growth in real GDP per capita (ADB 2019).

The strong association between urbanization and economic growth reflects a two-way relationship, with the two being "mutually self-reinforcing processes" (Martin and Ottaviano 1999). As countries develop and grow, economic activity and employment shift from agriculture to manufacturing and services activities. Locationally, this shift is accompanied by the growth of urban centers and the movement of workers to cities. This is because cities and their surrounding areas are where the production and exchange of many manufactured goods and services is most efficient, much innovation takes place, and many jobs are created. By enabling firms and workers to interact closely, cities generate increases in productivity through several channels, collectively known as "agglomeration economies." Box 1.1 describes the specific forces at work.

Given the importance of the urbanization–economic growth relationship, the urbanization process under way in India is a welcome and important development. While just 31.1% of India's population (377 million people) was urban in 2011, projections indicate that this share will increase to 50% of the population by the middle of the century, adding about 400 million people to India's cities.[1] For India to achieve its goal of becoming a high-income economy by 2047, it is crucial that India's cities fulfill their potential as engines of economic growth.

Of course, India's cities already contribute significantly to the economy. Thus, while cities in India occupy just 3% of the nation's land, their contribution to GDP is considerable—estimated to be 50%–60% of GDP in recent years—and the larger urban agglomerations and their surrounding areas,

---

[1] The numbers for 2011 are from the 2011 Census of India (ORGCC n.d.). The projections for 2050 are based on United Nations Department of Economic and Social Affairs (2018).

Box 1.1: What Accounts for Agglomeration Economies?

"Agglomeration economies" refers to the economic benefits that arise when firms and workers are located and operate in close physical proximity. The benefits arise because larger, denser locations make it more likely that workers will get jobs that are a good fit for their skills and needs, individuals and organizations will exchange ideas and knowledge, and resources are more efficiently shared—three mechanisms that are more conveniently referred to as matching, learning, and sharing, respectively (Duranton 2015, Behrens and Robert-Nicoud 2015).

First, larger (and denser) urban agglomerations allow more efficient matching between inputs and outputs. For example, workers are more likely to find a job that best suits their skills and abilities when there are many employers to choose from and vice versa.

Second, as large numbers of individuals and organizations interact, spillovers of ideas and knowledge are likely to increase and lead to learning. This learning can be in the form of cutting-edge ideas in high-tech industries or even in relatively standard products and production processes.

Finally, a larger urban agglomeration enables greater sharing of resources. In the labor market, for example, size allows for the development of both deeper individual specialization and widely available diverse expertise, thereby enhancing efficiencies from the division of labor. Software companies in Bengaluru, for example, benefit from a high concentration of law firms specializing in intellectual property rights. Similarly, economies of scale in the provision of physical and institutional infrastructure mean that such amenities are shared more efficiently among city dwellers than among those who live elsewhere.

Sources: Asian Development Bank. 2019. *Asian Development Outlook 2019 Update: Fostering Growth and Inclusion in Asia's Cities*; Asian Development Bank. 2021. *The Greater Mekong Subregion 2030 and Beyond: Integration, Upgrading, Cities, and Connectivity*; Duranton, G. 2015.*Growing Through Cities in Developing Countries*. Oxford University Press on behalf of the World Bank. https://openknowledge.worldbank.org/handle/10986/24808; Behrens, K., and F. Robert-Nicoud. 2015. Agglomeration Theory with Heterogeneous Agents. *Handbook of Regional and Urban Economics*. 5: 171–245.

---

such as India's National Capital Region, play a specially important role.[2] Indeed, an analysis of estimated district-level GDP suggests that each percentage point increase in a district's urban population share is associated with a 2.7% increase in value added.[3]

Further, India's cities are contributing considerably to generating better and more jobs. The share of "regular" wage workers in wage and salaried employment was 90.3% in large cities, compared to 75.6% in small cities and 33.4% in rural areas.[4] Regular jobs offer more employment stability and other nonwage benefits than casual wage work. Similarly, larger cities also tend to have a greater share of wage employment in enterprises with 10 or more workers (54.6% in larger cities, 46.8% in smaller cities, and 28.2% in rural areas), a proxy for employment in a formal sector enterprise. Finally, manufacturing and business services—subsectors associated with economic dynamism—account for a larger share of employment in urban areas, and large cities within them, than in nonurban areas.[5]

---

[2] According to the Central Statistical Organisation, 52.6% of net value added in India was generated in urban areas in 2011–2012. There are also other estimates based on different methodologies, such as computing the value added accruing to estimates of workers resident within a city. For example, the Ministry of Housing and Urban Poverty Alleviation (2016) reports an urban share of GDP close to 60%.

[3] District-level value added was estimated by first allocating 2011 sector-wise gross state value added (for 11 sectors) to constituent districts in proportion to each district's share of the state's sectoral employment, then summing the 11 sector-wise district gross value-added estimates to arrive at district value added. Employment data were obtained from the 2011 Census of India (ORGCC n.d.).

[4] Based on micro records of the National Statistics Office's Periodic Labour Force Survey (PLFS) of 2018–2019, which allows respondents in urban areas to be distinguished in terms of whether they belonged to cities with a population of 1.5 million or more in 2011.

[5] "Business services" as defined here includes transport and storage; information and communication; financial and insurance activities; real estate activities; professional, scientific, and technical activities; and administrative and support service activities.

Manufacturing and business services accounted for 49% of employment in large cities compared to 39% in smaller cities and just 14% in rural areas (Hasan 2022). Restricting attention to a narrower set of business services where agglomeration economies are likely to be especially important (that is, knowledge-oriented services such as those related to finance, consulting, and information technology), differences across rural areas and small and large cities remain quite important (accounting for 16.3% of employment in large cities compared with 7.4% in small cities and just 1.3% in rural areas).

There is also evidence to suggest that the economic dynamism of India's urban agglomerations comes at least in part from the forces underlying agglomeration economies. First, wages of otherwise similar workers tend to be higher in larger and/or denser cities, consistent with the idea that locating a large number of firms and workers near each other raises productivity.[6] For example, data from the Periodic Labour Force Survey for 2018–2019 show that even after controlling for age, gender, educational attainment, type of wage work (i.e., regular versus casual), and industry and occupation, full-time wage and salaried workers in cities with a population of 1.5 million or more averaged about 16% higher monthly earnings than their counterparts in smaller cities and 36% higher than counterparts in rural areas.[7] Second, consistent with the idea that urban agglomerations play a special role in fostering innovation, firms in India's larger cities are found to introduce product and process innovations and conduct research and development more often than their counterparts in smaller cities. Specifically, using geo-coded enterprise survey data on more than 8,000 enterprises across 207 Indian cities[8] and controlling for a wide range of city and firm characteristics, econometric analysis suggests that firms in a city twice as large as another are more likely to engage in product innovation, process innovation, and research and development by 18%, 10%, and 21%, respectively (Chen, Hasan, and Jiang 2021).

At the same time, harnessing the full economic potential of India's cities requires recognizing two issues. First, even as the forces of agglomeration raise the productivity of firms and workers in urban centers, thereby attracting still more entrepreneurs and workers and leading cities to grow larger, overcrowding and congestion can reduce the productivity of firms and workers. Cities must be managed appropriately to keep such issues from overwhelming the benefits of agglomeration.

Second, robust economic growth requires vibrancy in all types of cities, large and small. Cities are connected to one another and to the rural hinterland through flows of goods, services, and people. They form an urban system. Comprehensive economic growth depends not just on a few large cities but also on well-functioning market towns that specialize in marketing and distributing agricultural produce and on mid-size cities (ADB 2019). Box 1.2 describes the conceptual underpinning of both points, while Box 1.3 describes how cities are defined and distributed in India.

---

[6] To capture the productivity advantage of agglomeration, it is sufficient to show that firms pay higher nominal wages rather than real wages for workers with similar characteristics, such as age (a proxy for experience), gender, and educational attainment. This is because nominal wages reflect how much more firms are willing to pay in bigger cities to comparable workers (De La Roca and Puga 2016). Using real wages is appropriate when analyzing the welfare implications of different types of employment and studies of location choice.

[7] Admittedly, the findings above do not tell us about causality, due to the possibility that unobserved individual and locational characteristics may be important. For example, workers in larger cities may be paid better on account of higher unobserved human capital obtained through access to higher quality education. Similarly, more innovative entrepreneurs may choose to locate in larger cities in order to access a (typically) larger pool of skilled workers and better infrastructure. However, attempts to control for potential endogeneity using historic city size suggest that agglomeration effects are indeed present, though their magnitude can diminish dramatically upon the use of an instrumental variable strategy. See Chauvin et al. (2017) and Hasan et al. (2017) on agglomeration effects and wages.

[8] Geo-coded enterprise survey data are from the World Bank Enterprise Surveys. Cities are defined in terms of "natural cities" as defined in Asian Development Bank (ADB) (2019).

Box 1.2: Managing the Benefits and Costs of Agglomeration

There is a tension between agglomeration economies on one side and diseconomies from agglomeration on the other, such as those generated due to traffic congestion, air pollution, and unsanitary living conditions (Fujita, Krugman, and Venables 1999), and referred to in short as congestion. Congestion can take away the productivity of firms and workers, and thus the economic advantages of cities. The relationship between city size and net benefits of agglomeration can be represented as an inverted-U, as illustrated in Figure B1.2. The general idea is that agglomeration effects increase with city size until a point (such as P*) beyond which continued population expansion lessens, rather than amplifies, net agglomeration effects. While it is difficult to assess whether a given city is past its "optimal" size, local and national governments must act on tell-tale signs associated with diseconomies (i.e., congestion, pollution, slums, etc.).

Net Agglomeration Benefits and City Size

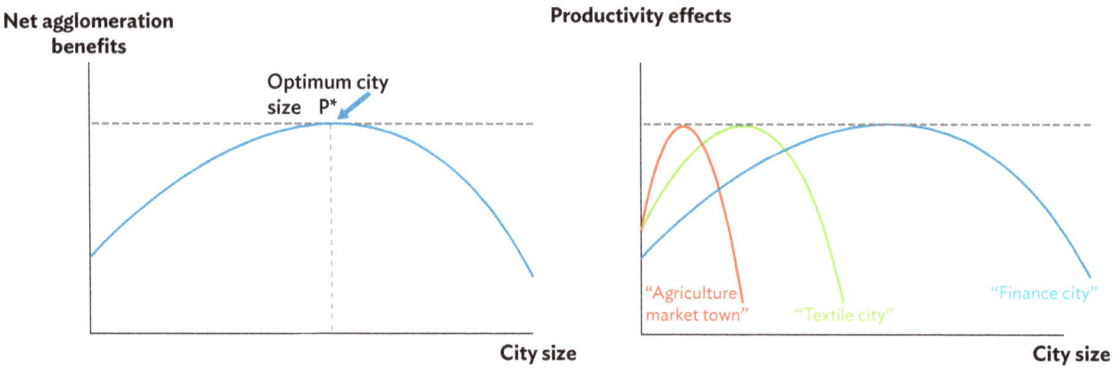

Source: Asian Development Bank. 2021. *The Greater Mekong Subregion 2030 and Beyond: Integration, Upgrading, Cities, and Connectivity*. Adapted from Fujita, M., and R. Ishii. 1998. Global Location Behavior and Organizational Dynamics of Japanese Electronics Firms and their Impact on Regional Economies. In A. D. Chandler, Jr. P. Hagstrom, and O. Solvell, eds. *The Dynamic Firm: The Role of Technology, Strategy, Organization and Regions*.

In addition, countries need vibrancy across the full range of cities—small, medium, and large. Two factors underlie this argument: (i) although all industries and activities benefit from agglomeration economies, they do so to different degrees; and (ii) the diseconomies of agglomeration, or congestion, tend to depend on city size regardless of industries. Thus, consider a city whose main economic activity involves the marketing and trading of agricultural produce versus another that specializes in knowledge-intensive processes such as finance and research and development. While both activities benefit from agglomeration economies, the benefits tend to be largest in knowledge-intensive industries. Thus, cities specializing in finance and/or research and development will typically be much larger than those specializing in agricultural produce. Because congestion will tend to accumulate equally in both cities—driven mainly by the number of people— the city specializing in marketing and trading agricultural produce will hit peak net agglomeration benefits at a fairly small size. Conversely, industries that benefit greatly from agglomeration forces are associated with a much larger optimal city size. The second panel of Figure B1.2 captures these relationships.[a]

[a] In addition to the fact that there are differences in the importance of agglomeration benefits across industries or activities, some industries or activities have greater potential than others for beneficial spillovers with one another. This implies that it is more efficient for cities to specialize in a few industries with significant mutual spillovers; otherwise, industries could generate excessive congestion and high land prices for one another.

Sources: Study team; Fujita, M., P. Krugman, and A. Venables. 1999. *The Spatial Economy: Cities, Regions, and International Trade*. MIT Press.

Box 1.3: India's Urban System

According to the 2011 Census of India, the country's urban system consists of 7,933 settlements, classified broadly as statutory (4,041) and census (3,892) towns (ORGCC n.d.). Urban agglomerations are a continuous spread of towns and outgrowths. The key definitions are as follows:

- **Statutory towns** are notified under law by the concerned state/union territory government and have local bodies such as municipal corporations, municipalities, and municipal committees, irrespective of their demographic characteristics.
- **Census towns** are settlements classified as urban in the census after they have met the following criteria: a minimum population of 5,000, at least 75% of the male "main workers" engaged in nonagricultural pursuits, and a population density of at least 400 people per square kilometer. Census towns are governed as villages and do not necessarily have urban local bodies.
- **Outgrowths** are viable units, such as a village, clearly identifiable in terms of their boundaries and locations. Outgrowths possess urban features in terms of infrastructure and amenities, such as all-weather roads, electricity, etc., and are physically contiguous with the core town of the urban agglomeration.
- **Urban agglomerations** are a continuous urban spread constituting a town and its adjoining outgrowths or two or more physically contiguous towns with or without outgrowths.

In 2011, 70.2% of India's total urban population was living in cities with over 100,000 people. Referred to as Class-I cities, these accounted for 44.7% of the country's total urban area. Within this group, the number and proportion of cities with over 1 million people have grown dramatically and will rise further. The number of cities with a 1-million-plus population was 35 in 2001 and 53 in 2011. Class II, III, and IV towns—i.e., those whose population ranges from 10,000 to 99,000—together make up 26% of India's total population and contribute over 44.2% to the country's total urban area.

Sources: Office of the Registrar General and Census Commissioner, India (ORGCC). n.d. 2011 Census of India. https://censusindia.gov.in/census.website/. NITI Aayog. 2021. Reforms in Urban Planning Capacity in India: Final Report. https://www.niti.gov.in/sites/default/files/2021-09/UrbanPlanningCapacity-in-India-16092021.pdf.

In practical terms, these issues imply that unless the urbanization process is managed well, greater urbanization may not realize its full potential for driving economic growth. Indeed, the urbanization process underway in the developing world provides many examples of cities that have become large but do not appear to foster or attract large numbers of particularly dynamic firms and serve as drivers of economic growth (Gollin, Jedwab, and Vollrath 2016).[9] Often, these cities are characterized by considerable traffic congestion and weak public transport systems that lead to fragmentation of the local labor markets. Further, air and water pollution and a proliferation of informal settlements where households live in unsanitary conditions and lack good access to decent educational and health facilities can short-circuit the process of accumulating human capital so vital to economic growth. Unplanned expansion of urban areas, underinvestments in crucial infrastructure, and rigidities in land-use regulations (encompassing restrictive zoning laws and outdated building bylaws) are a major reason for fragmentation of local labor markets as well as inadequacies in housing by restricting the supply of developed land accessible to major job centers and raising the costs of housing (and commercial properties). Further, rent control laws, meant to protect lower-income tenants, can exacerbate the problem. In the case of India, several commentators have noted that limited investment

---

[9] Gollin, Jedwab, and Vollrath (2016) note the case of two cities: Shanghai and Lagos. Both are large cities in countries with similar urbanization rates. However, the two cities' potential to deliver better economic outcomes is highly unlikely to be similar—one city is home to leading manufacturing firms that produce for global markets, the other city is characterized by firms that tend to produce primarily for local consumption.

in infrastructure, the prevalence of unsynchronized spatial and economic planning systems, and suboptimal land-use management are potential limits on the ability of cities to spur economic activity (see, in particular, Mathur 2016; Ahluwalia, Kanbur, and Mohanty 2014; World Bank 2013; and McKinsey Global Institute 2010).

Similarly, while many large, medium, and small-size cities are found in developing countries, especially larger ones, they do not form as dynamic an urban system as is the case in developed countries. Thus, while developed country urban systems are characterized by considerable sectoral and functional specialization, such systems in developing countries seem less specialized—for example, large cities in developed countries tend to be "nurseries" for producing new goods, which upon maturing relocate to smaller, more specialized cities; some cities tend to be more specialized in management-type functions; and others specialize in production-related functions (Duranton 2015).[10] Relatedly, while the largest cities in developing countries host firms engaged in various innovative activities (as noted above), the process of relocating production as products mature does not seem to be very prevalent. As a result, large cities in developing countries tend to host all types of producers and thus are prone to high degrees of congestion, while smaller cities are engaged in the production of traditional products and miss out on the invigorating effects that come from introducing the production of new products (Duranton 2015). Uneven distribution of basic urban infrastructure and inefficient and/or costly intercity transport systems are often the root causes of a weak urban system.

For India to realize the economic potential of its cities of all sizes requires investment in two complementary agendas. First, cities must be livable even as they become more densely populated. Ensuring livability of cities begins from the literal angle: they must be places where inhabitants' lives and livelihoods are protected from disasters. Due to climate change, cities are increasingly vulnerable to water stress, overheating, extreme weather events, and poor air quality. But they are also the population hubs with sufficient scale to pilot, test, and implement innovative technology- and policy-based climate solutions for the problems to which they have contributed. For adaptation to climate change, urban solutions include installing drainage and reinforced buildings and protecting urban biodiversity and green spaces.[11] For climate change mitigation, compact cities (a recurring theme throughout this report) that use green structures, transport, and resource management are important not only for economic connectivity and efficiency, but for limiting carbon emissions. In response to the diverse climate-related challenges faced across India (from devastating heatwaves in inland cities to the threat of flooding in coastal cities), city plans are being tailored to local vulnerabilities in climate action plans. Since 2019, the Ministry of Housing and Urban Affairs has assessed cities through its Climate Smart Cities Assessment Framework to steer cities toward more climate-resilient design and planning.

Access to amenities is also key to the livability agenda. Lack of affordable and fast public transport can lead to long, expensive commutes that restrict access to jobs, especially for low-income groups. Poor water supply and sanitation infrastructure impose health-related costs as well as gender-skewed time-related costs. Rigidities in land-use policies can constrain the supply of developable land,

---

[10] An illustration of specialization within the urban system is provided by Fujita and Ishii (1998): large Japanese multinationals produce their latest electronic products in sophisticated pilot plants near Tokyo and Osaka, while older generations of products are manufactured in less urbanized locations in Japan or in other countries, typically developing ones.

[11] There is also the issue of where new urban agglomerations should be encouraged. Virmani and Soni (2014) discuss how locations along rivers where large cities (with a population of 1 million or more) already exist may help decongest the large cities and present several advantages in terms of sustainability issues.

Box 1.4: Policies for Making Cities more Livable

The government has several initiatives for an urban sector transformation that ensure a better and more sustainable quality of life, reduce the carbon footprint, improve the capacity to adapt to climate change in a cost-effective way, promote mobilization of resources by urban local bodies, and enable cities to realize their and the country's economic potential. Some major schemes and priorities are as follows:

- **Improving universal coverage of basic urban services.** Schemes for this include national flagship programs such as the Smart Cities Mission, the *Pradhan Mantri Awas Yojana* (Housing for All), Atal Mission for Rejuvenation and Urban Transformation, Mass Urban Transit Systems in major cities, and *Swachh Bharat* (Clean India) Mission. These missions are targeted at building integrated and resilient urban infrastructure through improvements in water supply and sanitation including solid waste management, affordable and sustainable housing, enhanced tourism, and sustainable and comprehensive urban mobility.
- **Enhancing resources available to urban local governments.** The 15th Finance Commission has recommended that grants to rural and urban local bodies gradually move in favor of the latter. Within urban local bodies, the Commission has provided 50 "Million-Plus" cities a Challenge Fund (₹382 billion or approximately $5.2 billion at 2020 average exchange rates[a]), with almost one-third for achieving ambient air quality based on identified parameters, while the remaining two-thirds is for meeting service-level benchmarks for drinking water supply; rainwater harvesting; and water recycling, solid waste management, and sanitation. For cities with less than 1 million population, 40% of grants (₹829 billion or $11.2 billion) are untied while 60% of them are tied to the provision of drinking water, rainwater harvesting, solid waste management, and sanitation. Among the prerequisites for qualifying for the grants for urban local bodies, states must notify minimum floor rates of property taxes and then consistently improve their collection of property taxes in tandem with the growth rate of the state's own gross state domestic product. Grants have also been provided for improving health services (₹701 billion or $9.4 billion), incubating new cities (₹80 billion or $1.1 billion), and facilitating shared municipal services in urban areas (₹4.5 billion or $60.7 million).
- **Promoting a paradigm change in the area of urban planning.** To enable cities to meet their full potential as engines of growth, the budget for fiscal year 2022–2023 provides support to states for building the capacity of urban planning and for modernizing building by laws, implementing town planning schemes, and promoting transit-oriented development initiatives, among others.

[a] Indian rupees are converted into United States dollars using the average exchange rate of ₹74.13 per United States dollar in 2020, the year that the report of the 15th Finance Commission was published.
Source: Authors based on various official documents.

driving up costs for both businesses and workers and their families and encouraging sprawl.[12] The Government of India has several policies and schemes to address these issues (Box 1.4) and their speedy implementation is critical.

Second, cities must be good locations for enterprises' and entrepreneurs' investments. Cities attract investment when the publicly provided inputs that firms need are available locally—such as land in well-designed industrial and business parks, specialized infrastructure inputs (e.g., roads and bridges sufficient for the transport of heavy or oversized industrial products), and an ecosystem conducive to entrepreneurship covering not only the regulatory environment but also the availability of business

---

[12] For discussion of the interplay between land-use policies, urban sprawl, and economic outcomes see Sridhar (2019), Tewari et al. (2016), and World Bank (2013). See Patel and Pathak (2014) for a detailed discussion of how rigidities in land-use regulations in India cities can restrict the supply of formal housing and make it difficult to provide affordable housing to low-income households.

development services. Delivering such inputs is complex in India because the function of local economic development is often not with local governments but is exercised by state-level agencies such as state industrial development corporations; additionally, the agencies whose mandate it is to deliver the various publicly provided inputs that firms need are numerous and belong to different levels of government. If local governments are not incentivized to ensure that their cities are attractive to firms and not empowered to deliver on the needed inputs, the task of coordinating the work of different public agencies from different levels of government work can be formidable, making it difficult to ensure that firms operate in a conducive business environment. To this end, local governments in countries such as Brazil, the People's Republic of China, South Africa, and the United States are empowered to attract and hold firms.[13] Figure 1.1 attempts to capture the complexity of the coordination challenge by describing the many state-, regional-, and local-level agencies that jointly determine the business environment that firms face in a typical Indian city. Some of the agencies are departments of the state government that have a metropolitan or even state-wide scope, such as the industry, revenue, and town and country planning agencies. Others are institutions with a regional/local scope, such as the regional development authorities, special area development authorities, special purpose vehicles under the Smart Cities Mission, and urban improvement trusts. For example, water and drainage facilities are provided by the irrigation department, electricity is provided by a state public sector utility or a private firm or franchisee, waste is handled by the industrial authority and regulated by the state pollution control, and transport is often privately provided but regulated by a district transport authority. To the extent that stakeholders involved in these facilities work in sectoral silos, integrating planning or service provision in a city will be challenging.

To visualize the fragmentation of responsibilities across agencies, Figure 1.2 is a stylized description of the role of different agencies involved in planning and developing an industrial park.

For cities to achieve their full economic potential, good coordination across the public agencies involved in regulatory processes and provision of inputs key to economic activity is critical. Some Indian cities have instituted mechanisms to achieve the needed coordination, and it is important to understand how they have done so and the principles behind the mechanisms employed.

Scope of the Study

The study focused on developing a framework that states and their cities can use to foster greater economic growth and job creation. Two key study objectives included (i) identifying key bottlenecks that constrain Indian cities from fully realizing their potential as engines of growth; and (ii) developing implementable solutions to the bottlenecks, including workable structures of urban governance and mechanisms for coordinating spatial and economic planning. To meet the objectives, the study team reviewed literature and data, drew lessons from cities in India and internationally, and carried out extensive stakeholder consultations in 12 cities across seven Indian states. The outputs of the study are intended to be disseminated to state governments to encourage them to pursue initiatives for developing at the state and city levels policy frameworks that are appropriate for attracting and retaining business investment and creating jobs.

---

[13] For example, when the technology and e-commerce company Amazon announced in 2017 plans to build a second headquarters, scores of cities in Canada, Mexico, and the United States placed bids.

Figure 1.1: Generic Landscape of Urban Institutions' and Actors' Responsibilities in Indian Cities

State-Level Departments

Urban Development Department	Town and Country Planning Department	Industry Department	Revenue Department
• Focuses on matters related to development of physical infrastructure • Urban administration and coordination with the ULBs • In several cases, the state public works department is also part of the urban development department	• Focuses on matters related to master planning, land use, etc. • In some states, the TNCP department is a division of the Urban Development Department; in others it may be a stand-alone department	• Focuses on matters related to industrial development and attracting investments in the state. • In several states, the department also leads the economic growth of the state	Focuses on matters related to land transfer, and land allotment to public sector entities (such as ULBs, industries department, etc.)

Education Department	Water Resources
Planning, development, maintenance, and upkeep of primary, secondary, and professional educational institutes in the state	• Ensures water supply for residential, industrial, commercial, etc. uses, and related administrative support such as maintaining records • Looks after underground drainage connections, maintenance, and approvals for the services

City Administration

Urban Local Body	Development Authority
Focuses on city administration, including areas of building bylaws and local area construction norms, city cleanliness, water supply, infrastructure creation and upgrade, city cleanliness, waste management (including solid waste management, waste disposal, etc.), citizen services, etc.	• The city development authority focuses on creating physical infrastructure critical for the development of the city • The authority can sometime be part of the city administration or of the urban development authority of the state.

TNCP = Town and Country Planning, ULB = urban local body.
Note: The figure is a stylized description on the fragmentation of responsibilities in Indian cities, however several other responsibility structures are followed. The example is generic. The individual states' structures may vary depending on their own administrative organizations.
Source: Stakeholder consultations and the study team.

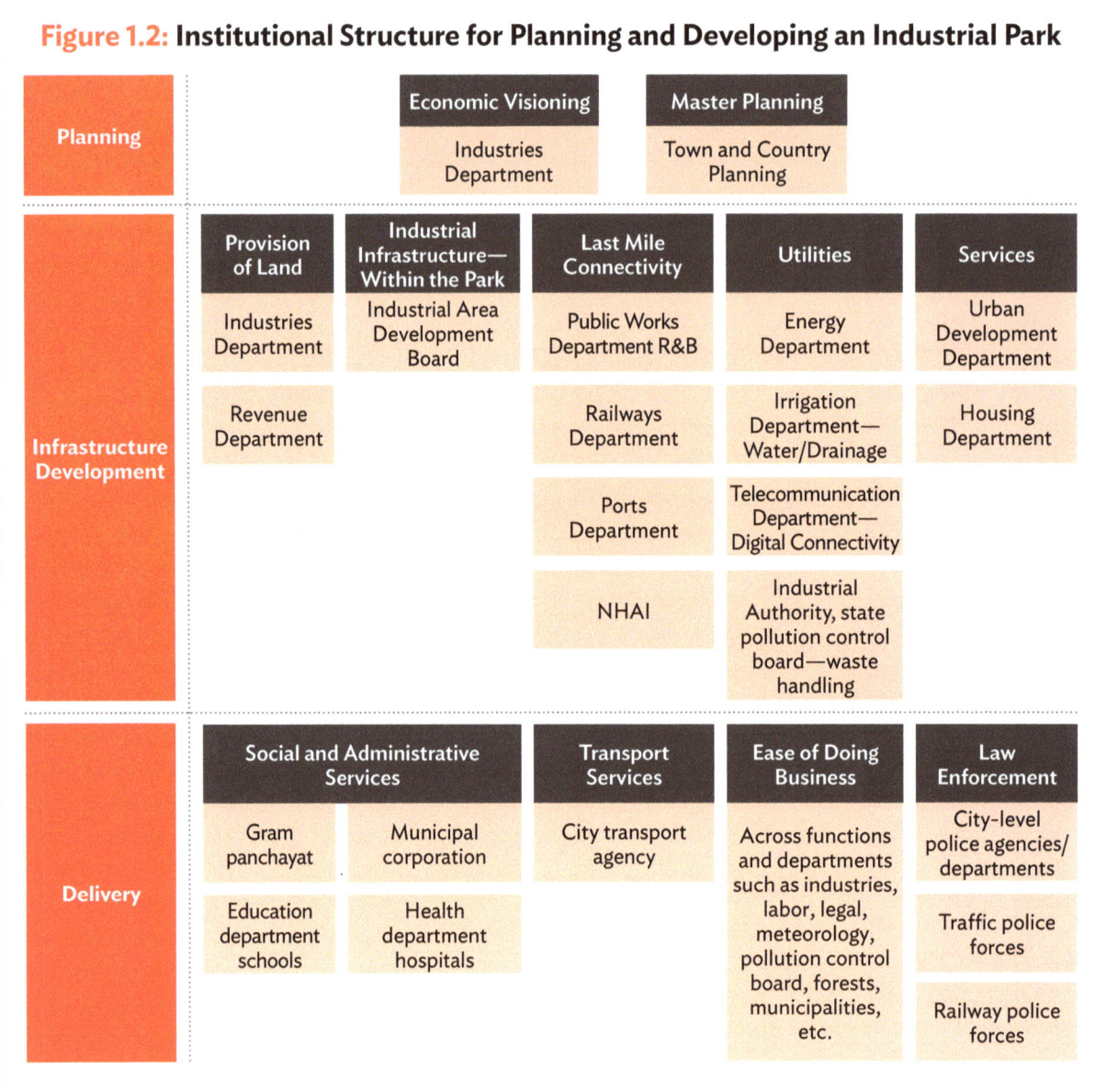

Figure 1.2: Institutional Structure for Planning and Developing an Industrial Park

NHAI = National Highway Authority of India, R&B = Roads and Buildings.
Note: The figure provides the general structure. Several states (and even separate areas in a state) may have different actors involved in planning and developing industrial parks; however, the general structure would be similar to this diagram.
Sources: Stakeholder consultations and the study team.

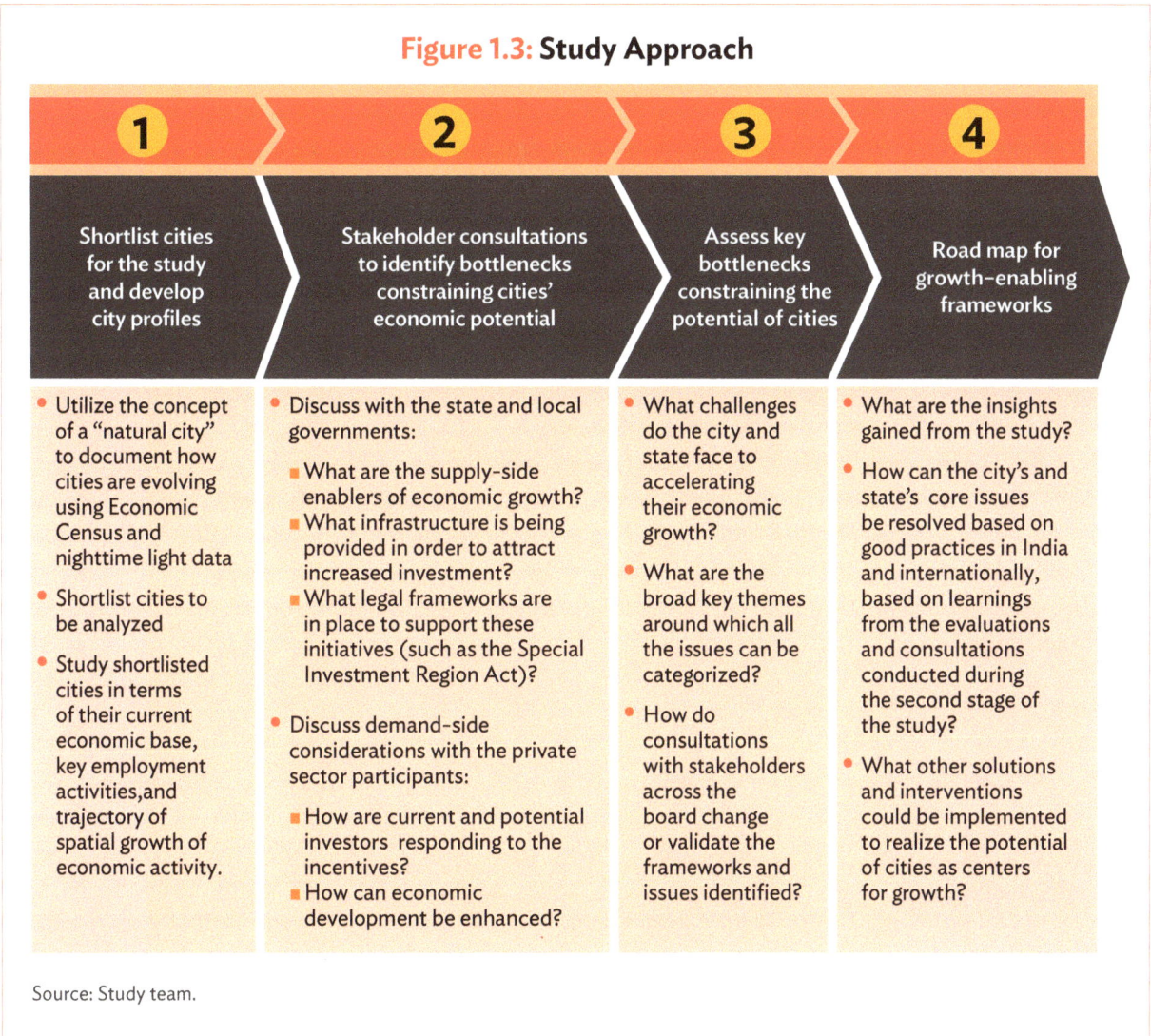

Figure 1.3: Study Approach

Source: Study team.

Approach of the Study

Figure 1.3 shows the four-step approach adopted for the study. Subsequent chapters are aligned with the four steps.

Shortlisting Cities and Developing City Profiles

Chapter 2 draws evidence from a wide variety of datasets (official statistics and a database constructed at the city level using satellite imagery). The concept of a "natural city" is used to document how cities are evolving (ADB 2019). The data allow urbanization to be defined in a way that captures the urbanization process as it unfolds beyond administrative city limits. They highlight how cities expand without regard for administrative boundaries and how clusters of cities in close proximity form larger conurbations. Chapter 2 also describes how the list of cities was determined for the purpose of analyzing growth bottlenecks and deriving a framework for better coordination of economic and spatial planning.

Consulting Stakeholders

To identify bottlenecks constraining the cities from realizing their full potential as "engines of growth" requires input from stakeholders. Thus, the study team consulted supply-side and demand-side actors in the shortlisted cities to obtain their specific and informed opinions and to better understand impediments to the cities' economic growth. Representatives of industries, prospective investors, industry associations, traders, government bodies, and others in the shortlisted cities were interviewed virtually and in person. More than 100 stakeholders from the seven states were consulted. The details are given in Chapter 4.

Assessing Key Bottlenecks Constraining Cities

The study team identified and analyzed the bottlenecks that constrain the cities from realizing their economic potential (Chapter 5). Five broad bottlenecks were identified: (i) lack of a common economic vision around which the different public agencies could coalesce; (ii) challenges related to land supply; (iii) master planning that is insufficiently aligned with economic goals, future land use, and infrastructure needs; (iv) inadequate institutional framework and capacity constraints; and (v) policies and regulations governing business.

Recommending Solutions

Questionnaires were prepared for different sets of respondents across the five bottlenecks to get insight into possible solutions, and responses were analyzed together with a mix of qualitative and quantitative data collected from secondary sources such as reports and statistical assessments and primary consultations.

Based on this, the study team developed a framework of possible solutions to the bottlenecks (Chapter 6). These were informed by learnings from Indian and international cities and are summarized in Table 1.1.

Table 1.1: Addressing Bottlenecks

1	2	3	4	5
Integrated Economic Vision	**Land Supply for Enabling Development**	**Integrated Master Planning**	**Institutional Integration and Capacity Building**	**Policies and Regulations Governing Business**
Visualize the economic activities that will drive the city's economy in the coming years.	Ensure land would be available for industries investing in the region.	Align master planning with economic goals and associated land use and infrastructure needs.	Foster institutional integration and build capacity in development and planning.	Develop of investment-friendly policies, and regulations.

Source: Study team.

References

Ahluwalia, I., R. Kanbur, and P. Mohanty. 2014. Challenges of Urbanisation in India: An Overview. In I. Ahluwalia, R. Kanbur, and P. Kumar Mohanty, eds. *Urbanisation in India: Challenges, Opportunities, and the Way Forward*. Sage. pp. 1–28.

Asian Development Bank (ADB). 2019. *Asian Development Outlook 2019 Update: Fostering Growth and Inclusion in Asia's Cities*.

———. 2021. *The Greater Mekong Subregion 2030 and Beyond: Integration, Upgrading, Cities, and Connectivity*.

Behrens, K., and F. Robert-Nicoud. 2015. Agglomeration Theory with Heterogeneous Agents. *Handbook of Regional and Urban Economics*. 5: 171–245.

Chauvin, J., E. Glaeser, Ma Yueran, and K. Tobio. 2017. What is Different about Urbanization in Rich and Poor Countries? Cities in Brazil, China, India, and the United States. *Journal of Urban Economics*. 98: 17–49.

Chen, Liming, R. Hasan, and Yi Jiang. 2021. Urban Agglomeration and Firm Innovation: Evidence from Asia. *The World Bank Economic Review*. October 2021. https://openknowledge.worldbank.org/handle/10986/36637E

De la Roca, J., and D. Puga. 2016. Learning by Working in Big Cities. *Working Papers* wp2013_1301, revised March 2016. Center for Monetary and Financial Studies.

Duranton, G. 2015. *Growing through Cities in Developing Countries*. Oxford University Press on behalf of the World Bank. https://openknowledge.worldbank.org/handle/10986/24808

Fujita, M., and R. Ishii. 1998. Global Location Behavior and Organizational Dynamics of Japanese Electronics Firms and their Impact on Regional Economies. In A. D. Chandler, Jr. P. Hagstrom, and O. Solvell, eds. *The Dynamic Firm: The Role of Technology, Strategy, Organization and Regions*. Oxford University Press.

Fujita, M., P. Krugman, and A. Venables. 1999. *The Spatial Economy: Cities, Regions, and International Trade*. MIT Press.

Gollin, D., R. Jedwab, and D. Vollrath. 2016. Urbanization with and without Industrialization. *Journal of Economic Growth*. 21(1) #2: 35–70.

Hasan, R. 2022. The Role of Cities in Ensuring Good Jobs. *Ideas for India*. 14 September. https://www.ideasforindia.in/topics/urbanisation/the-role-of-cities-in-ensuring-good-jobs.html.

Hasan, R., Yi Jiang, and R. Rafols. 2017. Urban Agglomeration Effects in India: Evidence from Town-Level Data. *Asian Development Review*. 34(2): 201–28.

Henderson, J. 2010. Cities and Development. *Journal of Regional Science*. 50 (1): 515–40.

Martin, P., and G. Ottaviano. 1999. Growing Locations: Industry Location in a Model of Endogenous Growth. *European Economic Review* 43(2).

Mathur, O. 2016. *Cities and the New Economic Vibrancy*. Institute of Social Sciences.

McKinsey Global Institute. 2010. *India's Urban Awakening: Building Inclusive Cities Sustaining Economic Growth*. http://www.indiaenvironmentportal.org.in/files/MGI_india_urbanization_fullreport.pdf (accessed 23 June 2018).

Ministry of Housing and Urban Poverty Alleviation (MHUPA). 2016. India Habitat III. National Report 2016. Government of India.

NITI Aayog. 2021. *Reforms in Urban Planning Capacity in India: Final Report*. https://www.niti.gov.in/sites/default/files/2021-09/UrbanPlanningCapacity-in-India-16092021.pdf

Office of the Registrar General and Census Commissioner, India (ORGCC). n.d. 2011 Census of India. https://censusindia.gov.in/census.website/ (accessed January–March 2022).

Patel, B., and V. Pathak. 2014. Integrating Redevelopment of Slums in City Planning. In I. Ahluwalia, R. Kanbur, and P. Mohanty, eds. *Urbanisation in India: Challenges, Opportunities, and the Way Forward*. Sage. pp. 260–96.

Sridhar, K. 2019. The Effect of Urban Land Use Regulations on Density: The Case of Selected Indian Cities. In S. Chakravorty and A. Palit, eds. *Seeking Middle Ground: Land, Markets and Public Policy*. Oxford University Press: 206–32.

Tewari, M., N. Godfrey, et al. 2016. Better Cities, Better Growth: India's Urban Opportunity. New Climate Economy Working Papers. World Resources Institute and Indian Council for Research on International Economic Relations. http://newclimateeconomy.report/workingpapers.

United Nations Department of Economic and Social Affairs (UN DESA). 2018. *World Urbanization Prospects: The 2018 Revision*. https://www.un.org/development/desa/publications/2018-revision-of-world-urbanization-prospects.html#:~:text=Today%2C%2055%25%20of%20the%20world's,increase%20to%2068%25%20by%202050.

Virmani, A., and V. Soni. 2014. Natural Cities. *Economic Political Weekly*. 49(19) 10 May. pp. 36–40.

World Bank. World Bank Enterprise Surveys. https://www.enterprisesurveys.org/en/enterprisesurveys.

———. 2013. Urbanization Beyond Municipal Boundaries: Nurturing Metropolitan Economies and Connecting Peri-Urban Areas in India. *Directions in Development*. World Bank. doi:10.1596/978-0-8213-9840-1. License: Creative Commons Attribution CC BY 3.0

Chapter 2

Shortlisting Cities for Study

Concept of Natural Cities Based on Nighttime Lights

Concepts Used to Define Cities

To understand the economic factors that drive a city, a focus on only statutory towns,[14] henceforth referred to as administrative cities, would be very limiting. This is because the economic activities of cities typically extend well beyond their statutory/administrative boundaries—for example, to industrial enclaves in peri-urban areas.

Two concepts of cities can capture this phenomenon.

- **Urban agglomeration (UA).** According to the 2011 Census of India (ORGCC n.d.), urban settlements include statutory towns and census towns[15] and outgrowths (areas outside the boundary of a town and within the "revenue limit" of a village or group of villages and possessing various urban features in terms of infrastructure and amenities).[16] A UA comprises contiguous urban areas consisting of a town and its adjoining "outgrowths" or two or more physically contiguous towns with or without their outgrowths. A UA consists of at least a statutory town and its total population (all constituents combined) of not less than 20,000.

- **Natural city (NC).** This concept is broader than the UA and draws on a study of cities across the Asia and Pacific region (ADB 2019).[17] It uses nighttime lights data from satellite images to capture the entire land area around a city (i.e., statutory towns with populations greater than 100,000 in 2000) with positive luminosity values. Positive luminosity values can be taken as a proxy measure that captures the presence of production and consumption activities associated with

---

[14] Statutory towns include locations with a municipal corporation, municipality, cantonment board, notified town area committee, town council, etc. The terms "town" and "city" are often used interchangeably.
[15] Census towns are settlements that meet three criteria: (i) population of at least 5,000, (ii) with 75% or more of the male population (working population in 1961 and 1971) engaged in nonagricultural pursuits, and (iii) a population density of at least 400 people per square kilometer. Census towns are administrative units formally classified as villages, but that satisfy the three foregoing criteria simultaneously.
[16] Examples of outgrowths include railway colonies, university campuses, and port areas.
[17] The study identifies more than 1,500 NCs across Asia and the Pacific using three main steps. First, human settlements are identified using nighttime light (NTL) satellite imagery from 1992 to 2016. Second, urban areas are distinguished by overlaying the NTL images with the geo-coded centers of cities that were identified in the database of the Global Rural Urban Mapping Project and had a population of 100,000 or more in 2000. Third, the entire contiguously illuminated area around the center is taken to define the NC. In this way, NTL data are used to track the footprints of NCs from 1992 to 2016. NTL imagery is derived from NTL images from the National Oceanic and Atmospheric Administration (https://ngdc.noaa.gov/eog/ [accessed 1 April 2017 and 10 August 2018] and since 2019 available from the Colorado School of Mines). The population of NCs is based on grid population data from LandScan Datasets of the Oak Ridge National Laboratory (https://landscan.ornl.gov/ [accessed 31 August 2017 and 31 August 2018]).

urban settlements. The scope of an NC could be broader than that of its corresponding UA. For example, an NC may encompass multiple small towns that are close to a large statutory town and not included in the UA, and include settlements defined as a village in the population census.[18]

For this study, the NC concept based on nighttime lights data was used to study spatial growth and economic activities with respect to the corresponding administrative city and its institutional framework to identify factors inhibiting these cities from realizing their full potential as engines of economic growth.

The Extent of Urbanization Using the Concept of Natural Cities

To appreciate the importance of different concepts of cities, consider the case of Indore (Figure 2.1). The left panel depicts the administrative city of Indore and the district of Indore and parts of adjoining districts.[19] The area includes several towns (shaded yellow) and villages (shaded green). The right panel shows the satellite image of Indore and surrounding areas. The expansive definition of the city, i.e., the NC of Indore, covers the area within the red boundary.

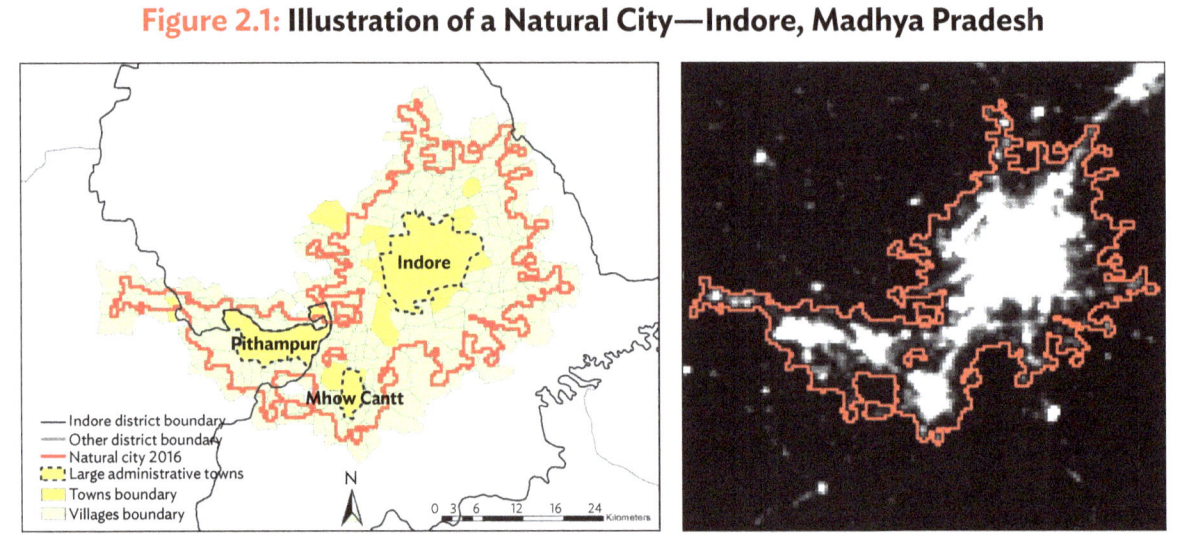

Figure 2.1: Illustration of a Natural City—Indore, Madhya Pradesh

Notes:
Panel 1: Indore's administrative boundaries are digitized from physical maps and conform to the 2011 Census of India data. See also World Bank (2016), described in detail in Li et al. (2016).
Panel 2: The dark areas within the natural city boundary depicted in red reflect areas (technically, "pixels") with low levels of luminosity in 2016.
Sources: ADB estimates using nighttime lights images from the National Oceanic and Atmospheric Administration https://ngdc.noaa.gov/eog/ (accessed 1 April 2017 and 10 August 2018 and since 2019 available from the Colorado School of Mines); India administrative shapefiles from World Bank. 2016. Spatial Database for South Asia. www.worldbank.org/spatialdatabase-southasia (accessed 7 September 2016).

---

[18] NCs have been mapped to subdistricts and towns and villages as feasible using administrative shapefiles for India from the World Bank's Spatial Database for South Asia (www.worldbank.org/spatialdatabase-southasia [accessed 7 September 2016]). The shapefiles used rely on subdistricts and towns and villages as captured by the 2011 Census of India.
[19] As mentioned in the notes to Figure 2.1, Indore's administrative boundaries are consistent with those utilized in 2011 Census of India data. The boundaries also apply to those in the 2001 census, reflecting the fact that administrative boundaries tend to be slow to change.

The concept of Indore's UA encompasses the administrative city of Indore and 10 adjoining towns, as defined by the Economic Census 2013–2014 (MOSPI 2018). Most of the towns are relatively small, with populations of about 9,000–19,000 people, other than Bangarda Chhota, which had more than 64,000 people in 2011. But the NC of Indore covers 20 towns and 265 villages likely to have urban types of economic activity, as captured by nighttime lights data (Figure 2.1). The largest of the 20 towns includes the administrative city of Indore, with a population of almost 2 million in 2011; Pithampur, with about 126,000; and Mhow Cantt, with 82,000. Pithampur is not in the district of Indore, but in Dhar district.

Table 2.1 shows how key industrial statistics for Indore differ depending on which definition of the city is considered. Specifically, the UA of Indore—which overlaps very closely with the Indore Municipal Corporation (which comprises about 90% of Indore UA's total population)—had almost 286,000 workers in various industries excluding agriculture and fishing, based on India Economic Census 2013–2014 data (MOSPI 2018).

In contrast, the NC of Indore had a little more than 390,000 people employed—about 37% more than the Indore UA. More importantly, the NC definition shows that Indore had a high employment share in manufacturing industries (30% versus 23% for the UA definition of a city). Moreover, based on the NC concept, there are many more large enterprises around the Indore area, and they contribute to employment in firms with 10 or more workers—a good proxy for formal employment. These industries are much more likely than smaller enterprises to be associated with future economic growth.

Table 2.1: Economic Structure of Indore Natural City Versus Indore Urban Agglomeration

Indore City Region	Total Employment (excluding agriculture and fishing)	Share of Manufacturing in Total Employment in Column 2	Share of Employment in Formal Employment (enterprises with 10 or more workers)	Number of Large Manufacturing Enterprises (enterprises with 100 or more workers)	Number of Large Business Services Enterprises (enterprises with 100 or more workers)
Urban Agglomeration	285,730	23%	17%	15	10
Natural City	390,617	30%	29%	92	15

Notes: The geographic units used to define the boundaries of Indore natural city in this table are towns and villages. Thus, there are slight differences with Indore natural city estimates in Chapter 3 as natural city boundaries in the latter are defined using subdistricts as the basic geographic unit of analysis.
Source: Asian Development Bank estimates using data from the India—Sixth Economic Census 2013–14 (MOSPI 2018) and the Asian Development Bank natural city database.

Selection of Cities

Twelve cities from seven geographically diverse states were selected as case studies for analyzing common growth bottlenecks and identifying frameworks for growth-enabling urban governance and planning (Table 2.2). The cities were selected through a top-down, three-tier approach: state, district, and city.

Table 2.2: The Twelve Selected Cities

State	City	Population Administrative City or Municipality	Natural City
Andhra Pradesh	Machilipatnam	169,892	203,402
Andhra Pradesh	Vijayawada	1,143,232	2,033,637
Assam	Guwahati	962,334	1,336,758
Gujarat	Navsari	171,109	350,899
Gujarat	Vadodara	1,752,371	2,394,552
Haryana	Hisar	307,024	633,574
Haryana	Sonipat[a]	289,333	NA
Madhya Pradesh	Dewas	289,550	329,538
Madhya Pradesh	Indore	1,994,397	2,947,734
Sikkim	Gangtok[b]	100,286	NA
Telangana	Nalgonda	154,326	188,178
Telangana	Warangal	704,570	829,423

NA = not applicable.
[a] Sonipat is encompassed within the Delhi natural city (NC) and thus has no NC of its own.
[b] NCs are defined in terms of their 2016 boundaries. No NC was defined for Gangtok because its population in 2000 was below 100,000, the threshold used to identify NCs in ADB (2019).
The geographic units used to define the boundaries of NCs in this table are towns and villages. Thus, there would be slight differences with NC estimates in Chapter 3 as NC boundaries in the latter are defined using subdistricts as the basic unit.
Sources: Office of the Registrar General and Census Commissioner, India (ORGCC). n.d. 2011 Census of India. https://censusindia.gov.in/census.website/; ADB Natural City Database (accessed January–March 2022).

State Selection

First, a set of five states was identified for regional diversity and based on indicators of urban population growth potential, economic output, business environment, sustainability, and infrastructure. From Central India, the state chosen was Madhya Pradesh; from North India, Haryana; from East and Northeast India, Sikkim; from Southern India, Telangana; and from Western India, Gujarat. Two other states were added to the list: Assam, which has the largest urban area in the northeastern region, and Andhra Pradesh. The East Coast Economic Corridor—India's first coastal economic corridor—runs through Andhra Pradesh, where maximizing synergies between industry and urbanization are a key planning feature.

District Selection

Districts were selected from the seven states based on a modification of an "economic potential index" developed by Roberts (2016). Table 2.3 lists the components of the index.[20] Using this mix of components ensured that key enablers for establishing modern businesses were available in the case study cities, without heavily favoring districts that were already performing well economically.

Table 2.3: Economic Potential Index Components

Dimension	Roberts' EPI (2016) Indicator	Modified EPI Indicator
Market Access	Travel time-based measure	Travel distance-based measure (see Hasan, Jiang, and Kundu [2018] for further details)
Economic Density	GDP per km^2	Not used
Level of Urbanization	% of population living in urban areas	% of population living in urban areas
Human Capital	Literacy rate	Secondary school completion rate of working age population
Local Transport Connectivity	Density of primary and secondary roads (length of roads in kilometers per 100 km^2)	% of main worker commutes done by automotive or locomotive means
Energy Access	Not used	Household electrification rate

EPI = economic potential index, GDP = gross domestic product, km^2 = square kilometer.
Notes: All indicators are district-level and based on population data from the 2011 Census of India.
Sources: Office of the Registrar General and Census Commissioner, India (ORGCC). n.d. 2011 Census of India. https://censusindia.gov.in/census.website/; Roberts, M. 2016. Identifying the Economic Potential of Indian Districts. *Policy Research Working Paper* 7623. World Bank; and Hasan R., Yi Jiang, and D. Kundu. 2018. *The Growth of Indian Cities and "Good" Jobs: Evidence from the 2000s*. India Policy Forum, NCAER.

The indicators of these components are standardized and combined into an index in a non-substitutable fashion, as shown in Table 2.4. This is because (i) the components are likely complementary (rather than substitutive) in creating an environment that is conducive to economic growth, and (ii) economic potential (particularly for manufacturing and modern services) is likely to be constrained if a district lags in any one indicator.

Table 2.4: Thresholds for Economic Potential Index Ratings

Rating	Threshold
Very High	z-score ≥ 1 for all indicators
High	z-score ≥ 0 for all indicators, z-score < 1 for at least one indicator
Moderate	z-score ≥ −1 for all indicators, z-score < 0 for at least one indicator
Low	z-score ≥ −1.5 for all indicators, z-score < −1 for at least one indicator
Very Low	z-score ≤ −1.5 for at least one indicator

Source: Study team.

---

[20] To assess growth potential at the district level, the study team drew on the economic potential index of Roberts (2016). While our approach is similar to his, we made two major changes. First, in addition to selecting different indicators for market access, human capital, and local transport connectivity, we substituted energy access for the economic density dimension. Second, while we standardized the indicators into z-scores as Roberts (2016) did, our index is defined differently. Rather than taking the average of five indicator z-scores (and scaling that average score so that the maximum score is 100), we used the z-scores directly.

City Selection

According to the 2011 Census of India, 115 cities had more than 100,000 inhabitants in districts of the seven states with at least "moderate" economic potential. To arrive at a final list of 1–2 cities per state that reflect the study's focus on emerging urban centers, cities that had the following characteristics were excluded:

(i)   cities with populations greater than 3 million and that are immediate neighbors of megacities (Delhi);

(ii) cities that rely heavily on mining;

(iii) cities with shares of both formal employment (firms with 10 or more workers) and manufacturing employment in the bottom quintile of Indian cities; and

(iv) cities in NCs that did not specialize in manufacturing or modern business services.

After allowing exceptions from the foregoing exclusions, to allow the inclusion of cities in Assam and Sikkim, the criteria narrowed the list to 47 cities, from which one city from Sikkim and Assam and two cities from the other five states were selected to provide variety in city size (one small city with population less than 300,000, one large city with population greater than 300,000). Within each state and city size group, the city with the highest district economic potential index was selected, with the NC's share of employment in manufacturing serving as a tiebreaker. The result of this process is listed in Table 2.5.

Table 2.5: Selected Cities

Region	State	City
Central	Madhya Pradesh	Dewas
		Indore
Northeastern	Assam	Guwahati
	Sikkim	Gangtok
Northern	Haryana	Hisar
		Sonipat
Southern	Andhra Pradesh	Machilipatnam
		Vijayawada
Telangana		Nalgonda
		Warangal
Western	Gujarat	Navsari
		Vadodara

Source: Study team.

References

Asian Development Bank (ADB). 2019. *Asian Development Outlook 2019 Update: Fostering Growth and Inclusion in Asia's Cities.*

———. ADB Natural City Database (accessed January–March 2022).

Hasan R., Yi Jiang, and D. Kundu. 2018. *The Growth of Indian Cities and "Good" Jobs: Evidence from the 2000s*. India Policy Forum, NCAER.

Li, Yue; M. Rama; V. Galdo; and M. Pinto. 2016. A Spatial Database for South Asia. *Working Paper*. World Bank. https://collaboration.worldbank.org/content/sites/collaboration-for-development/en/groups/research-partnership-for-sustainable-urban-development/groups/spatial-development-research/documents.entry.html/2016/05/24/a_spatial_databasef-qJjy.html.

Ministry of Statistics and Programme Implementation (MOSPI), Government of India. 2018. *India—Sixth Economic Census 2013–14*. National Data Archive. http://microdata.gov.in/nada43/index.php/catalog/47.

———. Primary Census Abstract Census 2011.

National Oceanic and Atmospheric Administration (NOAA). https://ngdc.noaa.gov/eog/ (accessed 1 April 2017 and 10 August 2018). Nighttime light data are available since 2019 from the Colorado School of Mines.

Office of the Registrar General and Census Commissioner, India (ORGCC). n.d. 2011 Census of India. https://censusindia.gov.in/census.website/ (accessed January–March 2022).

Roberts, M. 2016. Identifying the Economic Potential of Indian Districts. *Policy Research Working Paper* 7623. World Bank.

World Bank. 2016. Spatial Database for South Asia. www.worldbank.org/spatialdatabase-southasia (accessed 7 September 2016).

Chapter 3

City Profiles—Economic Activity and Spatial Growth

This chapter provides a brief profile of each shortlisted city, focusing on the structure of city-level economic activity and spatial growth. Most city profiles are presented at two levels—the administrative city (AC) and the natural city (NC).[21] The NC concept is used to examine spatial growth of the city, i.e., how the "urban footprint" of cities has evolved from 2000 to 2016.[22] The chapter also briefly outlines the state of existing and planned economic development. The profiles were developed using state economic surveys as available (e.g., DES n.d.), micro-records of the India Economic Censuses 2013–14, and data on NCs for 2000 and 2016 from ADB (2019).[23]

Dewas

Brief Demographic Profile

Dewas is near Indore city in Madhya Pradesh and had a population of 289,550 according to the 2011 Census of India and a literacy rate of 84.6%—including a male literacy rate of 91.1% and female literacy rate of 77.7% (ORGCC n.d.).

Economic Profile and Spatial Growth

Manufacturing is an important component of the Dewas economy. The Economic Census 2013–14 indicated that the secondary sector contributes 42.7% of the AC's employment, followed by the tertiary (53.8%) and primary (3.4%) sectors.[24] Within the secondary sector, manufacturing was the major contributor to the city's economy. Key manufacturing subsectors in Dewas were metal-based

---

[21] Conceptually, an AC should cover only the statutory town whereas an NC in most cases comprises multiple towns and villages (as shown in Chapter 2). While the administrative boundaries of cities are best defined using the relevant statutory towns as the basic unit of analysis, due to data constraints, this chapter adopts the subdistrict as the basic geographic unit in determining the administrative boundaries of ACs and NCs. Thus, AC-related estimates of economic activity provided here pertain to the entire subdistrict where the AC is located. In the same way, the NC boundary of the project cities was also determined using the subdistrict as the basic unit. If a portion of the subdistrict is actually part of the NC, the entire subdistrict is counted in the NC data. If a subdistrict cuts across two or more adjacent NCs, it is assigned to the NC that accounts for the highest share of its area.
[22] Based on a comparison of information from the 2001 and 2011 censuses, the AC areas of Dewas, Gangtok, Hisar, Indore, Machilipatnam, and Nalgonda were unchanged; the AC areas of Guwahati, Navsari, Sonipat, Vadodara, and Warangal increased due to changes in jurisdiction; and the AC area of Vijayawada increased due to revised computation by the 2011 Census of India.
[23] This chapter relies mainly on microdata from the economic censuses of 2013–14 and 1998 (MOSPI 2018b, 2018a) to examine employment patterns across sectors and location of establishments. The locations are matched to subdistricts reported in the 2011 Census of India. (ORGCC n.d. https://censusindia.gov.in/census.website). The India Economic Census' coverage of agriculture, forestry, and fishing excludes crop production and plantation. However, as the focus is on urban areas, this should not be a significant limitation.
[24] Because Dewas NC and AC are in the same subdistrict (Dewas subdistrict), estimates of employment from the Economic Census 2013–14—which are generated at the subdistrict level in this chapter—are the same for the two.

City Profiles—Economic Activity and Spatial Growth

industry (sheet metal processing and gun metal); engineering manufacturing (automobile parts and fabrication mechanical units); agro- and food-based products (soy and wheat); rubber- and plastic-based manufacturing; and textile (cotton and synthetic) manufacturing.

The Dewas industrial belt occupies about 1,600 hectares (4,000 acres). Traditional crafts and handicrafts such as shoes, synthetic carpets, and leather work (e.g., bags, belts, ladies' purses, shoes, coats, and briefcases) remain important in the Dewas economy. Dewas is also a major Indian center for soy bean processing industries and is known as the soy capital of India. Many high-tech industries have been set up in Dewas for extracting oil from soybeans (MMSME n.d.).

The urban footprint of Dewas has evolved considerably since 2000. Figure 3.1 depicts the city of Dewas and its AC, much of the district of Dewas, and parts of adjoining districts. The area shaded green was the AC according to the 2011 Census of India; the extended area, within the red boundary, was Dewas NC in 2000 (left panel) and 2016 (right panel). The NC area grew 103.5% from 2000 to 2016. Figure 3.1 illustrates how the NC evolved from 2000 to 2016, encompassing one town and 224 villages mostly to the northeast and southwest.

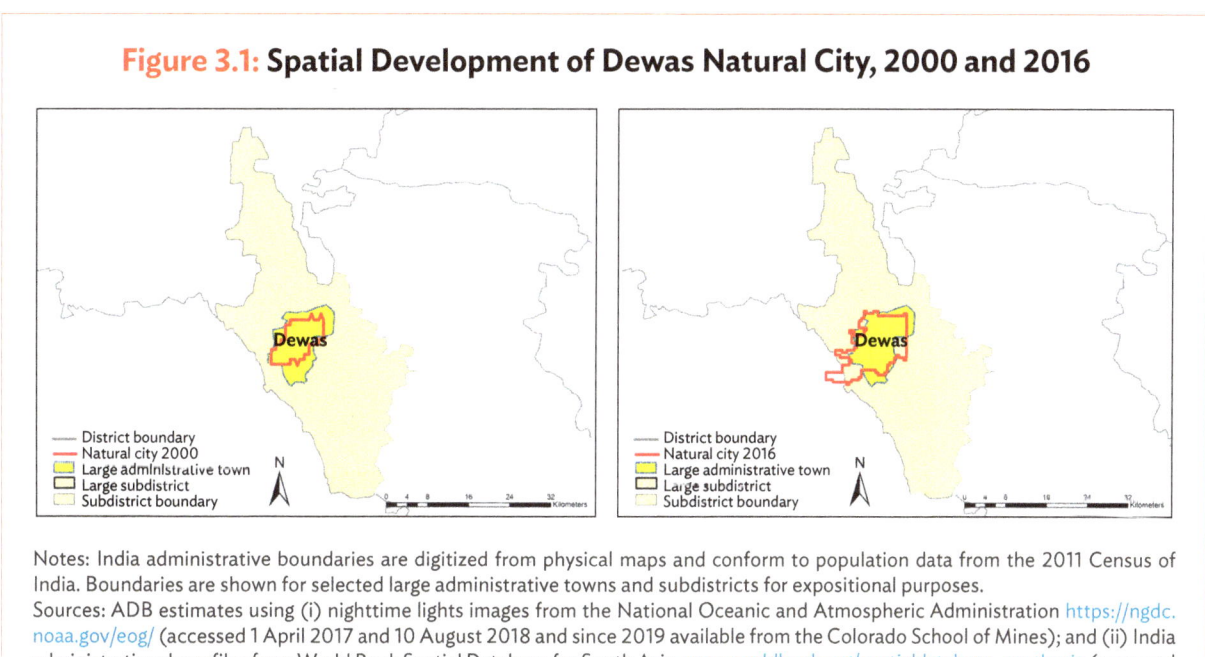

Figure 3.1: Spatial Development of Dewas Natural City, 2000 and 2016

Notes: India administrative boundaries are digitized from physical maps and conform to population data from the 2011 Census of India. Boundaries are shown for selected large administrative towns and subdistricts for expositional purposes.
Sources: ADB estimates using (i) nighttime lights images from the National Oceanic and Atmospheric Administration https://ngdc.noaa.gov/eog/ (accessed 1 April 2017 and 10 August 2018 and since 2019 available from the Colorado School of Mines); and (ii) India administrative shapefiles from World Bank Spatial Database for South Asia. www.worldbank.org/spatialdatabase-southasia (accessed 7 September 2016).

The potential for Dewas as a manufacturing hub could be realized by developing and implementing a vision of attracting a variety of industries. This would entail a strong focus on policies and regulations conducive for the development of manufacturing and the related social infrastructure, including real estate, to ensure the right infrastructure and facilities are available for living, playing, and working.

Gangtok

Brief Demographic Profile

Gangtok is the capital of Sikkim state, and had a population of 100,286 according to the 2011 Census of India and a literacy rate of 89.3% (with a male literacy rate of 92.8% and female literacy rate of 85.5%).

Economic Profile and Spatial Growth

Gangtok is the commercial, administrative, and educational center of Sikkim state. Key manufacturing subsectors in Gangtok are chemical and chemical-based industries (pharmaceuticals, cosmetics, and distillery products); agro- and food-based industries (breweries and food processing); textiles and apparel; and paper and cottage industries (handicrafts and wood and bamboo products such as furniture and decorative items). Pharmaceutical manufacturers in the city enjoy excise benefits from the central government. Glenmark Private Company, Sun Pharma, and Macleods Pharmaceuticals have a major part in the contribution of Gangtok city's secondary sector to the state's gross value added.

Figure 3.2 depicts the AC of Gangtok (colored yellow) according to the 2011 Census of India. The right side of the figure overlays the Gangtok AC with nighttime lights data, showing that very few luminous areas lie outside the boundaries of the Gangtok AC.

Gangtok's main challenge is to improve urban infrastructure and come up with new solutions for mobility, urban services delivery, and real estate development. This would entail enacting legislations that enable simpler acquisition of land; policies conducive to business development; and regulations for attracting investments to the services sector, such as hospitality, healthcare, and education. A comprehensive plan combining economic growth, urban sector development, and development of mobility infrastructure is needed.

Figure 3.2: Gangtok Administrative City

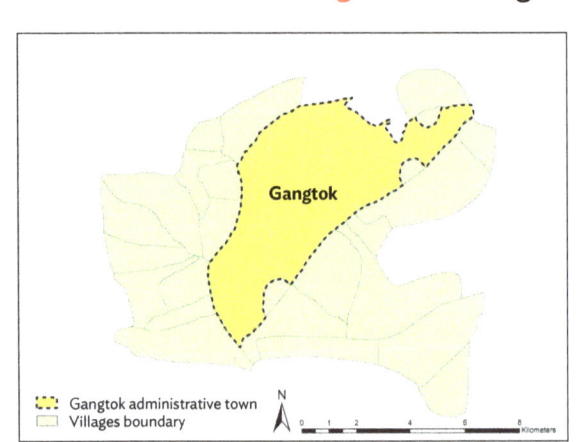 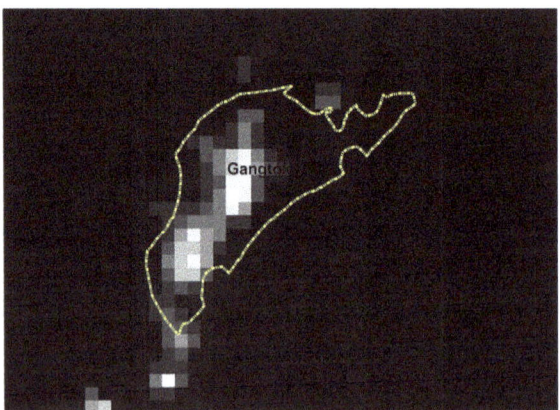

Notes: Administrative boundaries are digitized from physical maps and conform to the population data of the 2011 Census of India. Boundaries are shown for selected large administrative towns and subdistricts for expositional purposes.
Sources: ADB estimates using (i) nighttime lights images from the National Oceanic and Atmospheric Administration https://ngdc.noaa.gov/eog/ (accessed 1 April 2017 and 10 August 2018 and since 2019 available from the Colorado School of Mines); and (ii) India administrative shapefiles from World Bank Spatial Database for South Asia. www.worldbank.org/spatialdatabase-southasia (accessed 7 September 2016).

Guwahati

Brief Demographic Profile

Guwahati is the largest city in the state of Assam. The city had a population of 962,334 as per the 2011 Census of India and a literacy rate of 91.5% (with a male literacy rate of 94.2% and female literacy rate of 88.5%).

Economic Profile and Spatial Growth

Services is the dominant sector in driving the economic growth of Guwahati AC.[25] Guwahati AC contributes more than 50% of Kamrup Metropolitan District's economy.[26] Based on the Economic Census 2013–14, the tertiary sector accounted for a major share (about 83.0%) of the city's employment, followed by the secondary (16.0%) and primary (1.0%) sectors. Among the tertiary subsectors, the highest shares of the city's employment were in trade (41.0%) followed by professional and business services (14.6%).[27]

All of the successful industrial manufacturing subsectors in Guwahati are based on value chains within the northeastern region. Raw materials are either procured from within Assam or from states such as Meghalaya and Tripura. Key manufacturing industries in Guwahati in terms of number of establishments and employees include petrochemicals; food processing (processed and blended tea); and chemical manufacturing (paints, varnishes, and soaps and detergents). Tea manufacturing and processing is an important activity in Guwahati. The Guwahati Tea Auction Centre is the world's largest "crush, curl, and tear" tea auction center and the second largest in total tea auctioned. Paper manufacturing and petrochemical industries also contribute significantly to Guwahati's economy. The Guwahati refinery is an important manufacturing industry in the city.[28]

The urban footprint of Guwahati NC has evolved considerably since 2000. Figure 3.3 depicts the Guwahati AC, much of the district of Guwahati, and parts of adjoining districts. The area shaded green was the AC as per the 2011 Census of India; the extended area, within the red boundary, was the NC in 2000 (left panel) and 2016 (right panel). The NC grew 176.8% from 2000 to 2016 and, by 2016, the NC area was substantially larger than Guwahati's AC. Also, from 2000 to 2016, the NC population grew an average of 2.9% annually.

Figure 3.3 illustrates how the NC's spatial footprint had evolved since 2000. The NC had reached beyond Guwahati city's administrative borders by 66%, primarily to the north, west, and southeast. In 2016, the NC spanned 27 towns and 1,114 villages in four districts (Darrang, Kamrup Metropolitan, Kamrup Rural, and Ribhoi).

---

[25] Economic Census estimates for Guwahati AC cover the subdistricts of Guwahati and Dispur.
[26] Information collected based on stakeholder consultations conducted during 8–10 December 2021.
[27] Includes financial intermediation, insurance and pension funding, real estate, other business activities, and other services auxiliary to financial services.
[28] Further details are available at https://en.wikipedia.org/wiki/Guwahati.

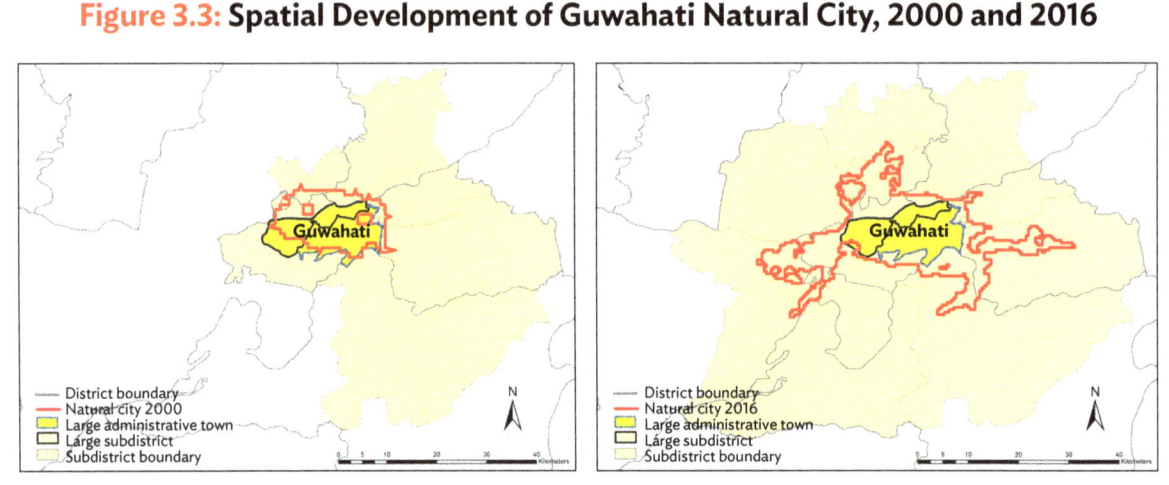

Figure 3.3: **Spatial Development of Guwahati Natural City, 2000 and 2016**

Notes: Administrative boundaries are digitized from physical maps and conform to population data from the 2011 Census of India. Boundaries are shown for selected large administrative towns and subdistricts for expositional purposes.
Sources: ADB estimates using (i) nighttime lights images from the National Oceanic and Atmospheric Administration https://ngdc.noaa.gov/eog/ (accessed 1 April 2017 and 10 August 2018 and since 2019 available from the Colorado School of Mines); and (ii) India administrative shapefiles from World Bank Spatial Database for South Asia. www.worldbank.org/spatialdatabase-southasia (accessed 7 September 2016).

Economic growth has been led by manufacturing in Guwahati NC and services within Guwahati AC.[29] The NC's spatial footprint increased due to relocation and development of formal and large-scale manufacturing activities outside the AC boundary. In 2013, the AC had almost 393,000 workers in manufacturing and services[30] (excluding public administration and defense) and the NC had almost 555,000 people employed—about 41.2% more than the Guwahati AC. Guwahati NC had a higher share of employment in manufacturing (15.3%) than the AC (9.8%). In 2013, Guwahati NC had many more manufacturing establishments than its AC, with the NC reporting a more than two-fold rise, during the same period.

The prime commercial clusters in Guwahati are concentrated around the central business district and along the Guwahati–Shillong Road. A majority of the industries within the Guwahati Metropolitan District Area limits are isolated small and medium-sized enterprises while major investments and developments are outside Guwahati (in a radius of more than 30 kilometers from the city center), mainly in areas such as Chaygam, Nagaberra, and Palasbari. Industrial parks such as the Brahmaputra Industrial Park, Export Promotion and Industrial Park, and Japanese Industrial Park are upcoming industrial nodes beyond the AC. Many other industries are also concentrated outside the periphery of Guwahati AC.[31]

Guwahati is the largest city in the northeastern region and should be positioned as a "Gateway to the North-East" and a hub where service industries are incentivized to relocate and expand. This has to be supported by high-quality connectivity and social infrastructure along with an evolved real estate sector catering to all sections of the society and providing a high-quality lifestyle.

---

[29] Economic census estimates for Guwahati NC cover 13 subdistricts versus only two subdistricts for Guwahati AC.
[30] "Services" includes electricity, gas, and water supply, as well as construction, although these subsectors are usually classified as "industries."
[31] Based on the stakeholder consultations held by the study team through December 2021 in Assam.

City Profiles—Economic Activity and Spatial Growth

Hisar

Brief Demographic Profile

Hisar is an administrative center for several key departments in the state of Haryana. Hisar had a population of 307,024 as per the 2011 Census of India and a literacy rate of 84.6% (with a male literacy rate of 90.2% and female literacy rate of 78.1%).

Economic Profile and Spatial Growth

The economy of Hisar largely depends on the tertiary sector. The Economic Census 2013–14 indicated that the tertiary sector accounted for 63.1% of the AC's employment, followed by the secondary (21.0%) and primary (15.8%) sectors.[32] Among subsectors, trade (22.7%) had the highest share of Hisar AC's employment, followed by manufacturing (18.6%), education and health (16.8%), and agriculture (15.8%).[33] The city's major manufacturing activity is concentrated around food processing, metal products fabrication, and textile industries.

The public sector is the primary employer of the city's working population because of its many state government department and agency headquarters; a large Indian Army base; major border security force bases for Northern India; and India's first dedicated maintenance, repair, and overhaul airbase.

Historically, the city's development has been led by a single industrial conglomerate (the Jindal Group) and its ancillaries (located in the city, the Jindal Group' ancestral base). All the major developments in the social infrastructure space are led by the government or the industrial conglomerate.

Figure 3.4 shows Hisar AC, much of the district of Hisar, and parts of adjoining districts. The area shaded green was the AC according to the 2011 Census of India; the extended area, within the red boundary, was the NC in 2000 (left panel) and 2016 (right panel). The NC grew 117.5% from 2000 to 2016. By 2016, the NC area was substantially larger than that of its AC. From 2000 to 2016, the NC population grew an average of 3.8% annually.

Figure 3.4 illustrates how the NC's urban expansion evolved since 2000. The expansion of the NC was not constrained by administrative boundaries. By 2016, the NC had extended beyond the AC's administrative borders, mainly to the northwest and southeast. In 2016, the NC spanned 10 towns and 229 villages in two districts (Bhiwani and Hisar).

---

[32] Economic Census estimates for Hisar AC cover the subdistrict of Hisar.
[33] Includes agriculture, hunting, and forestry.

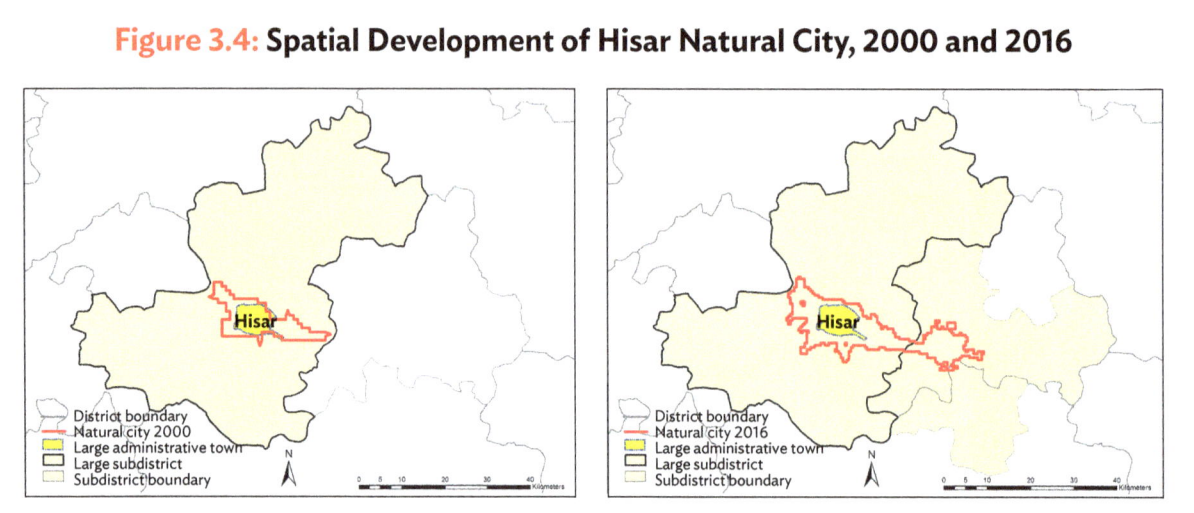

Figure 3.4: **Spatial Development of Hisar Natural City, 2000 and 2016**

Notes: India administrative boundaries are digitized from physical maps and conform to population data from the 2011 Census of India. Boundaries are shown for selected large administrative towns and subdistricts for expositional purposes.
Sources: ADB estimates using (i) nighttime lights images from the National Oceanic and Atmospheric Administration https://ngdc.noaa.gov/eog/ (accessed 1 April 2017 and 10 August 2018 and since 2019 available from the Colorado School of Mines); and (ii) India administrative shapefiles from World Bank Spatial Database for South Asia. www.worldbank.org/spatialdatabase-southasia (accessed 7 September 2016).

Spatial growth has led to increased manufacturing activity outside Hisar AC. The expansion has resulted from relocation and development of formal and large-scale manufacturing activities outside the AC. In 2013, the AC had almost 95,000 workers in manufacturing and services (excluding public administration and defense),[34] whereas the NC had almost 128,000, i.e., 34.8% more than the AC.[35] The NC employment share in manufacturing was 18.4% versus 18.6% for the AC. The NC had 71 large enterprises (employing 100 or more people), many more than the AC at 51.

Because Hisar hosts many public sector enterprises (including state government departments and agencies, defense establishments, and India's first dedicated maintenance, repair, and overhaul facility for aviation), the city should focus on further developing its strengths in the public and related sectors.

Indore

Brief Demographic Profile

Indore is the commercial hub for the state of Madhya Pradesh. Indore had a population of 1,994,397 according to the 2011 Census of India and a literacy rate of 85.9% (with a male literacy rate of 90.0% and female literacy rate of 81.0%).

---

[34] "Services" here also includes electricity, gas, and water supply as well as construction, although these subsectors are usually classified as "industries."
[35] Economic Census estimates for Hisar NC cover three subdistricts as against only one covered under Hisar AC.

Economic Profile and Spatial Growth

Indore district's gross state domestic product in fiscal year 2017–2018 stood at ₹473 billion. The city of Indore constituted more than half of that (about 58.2%). Nearly three-quarters (74.3%) of the AC's employment has been in the tertiary (largest) sector followed by the secondary sector at 24.6% and primary sector at 1.1%.[36] Employment in trade and hotels contributed the highest share at 38.7% followed by manufacturing at 23.1%. In terms of the number of establishments and workers, key manufacturing subsectors in Indore included chemicals; textiles; primary and fabricated metal manufacturing (parts made of alloys, steel, and automotive industries); and food processing industries. Metal and food processing industries were also an integral part of Indore's economy, accounting for 23% of establishments and of employees in the city.

The urban footprint of Indore NC has evolved considerably since 2000. Figure 3.5 depicts the city of Indore, much of the district of Indore, and parts of adjoining districts. The area shaded green was Indore AC as per the 2011 Census of India. The extended area, which lies within the red boundary, was the NC in 2000 (left panel) and 2016 (right panel). The NC area grew considerably from 2000 to 2016, by 196.3%—by 2016, the NC was substantially larger than its administrative counterpart, the AC. Also, from 2000 to 2016, the NC population grew by an average of 4.3% annually. Figure 3.5 illustrates how Indore NC evolved spatially since 2000. The NC reached beyond Indore city's administrative borders, mostly to the northeast (Dewas) and southwest (Pithampur and Mhow Cantt). The extensive scope of the NC involved multiple administrative units. In 2016, Indore NC spanned 28 towns and 1,074 villages in two districts (Dhar and Indore).

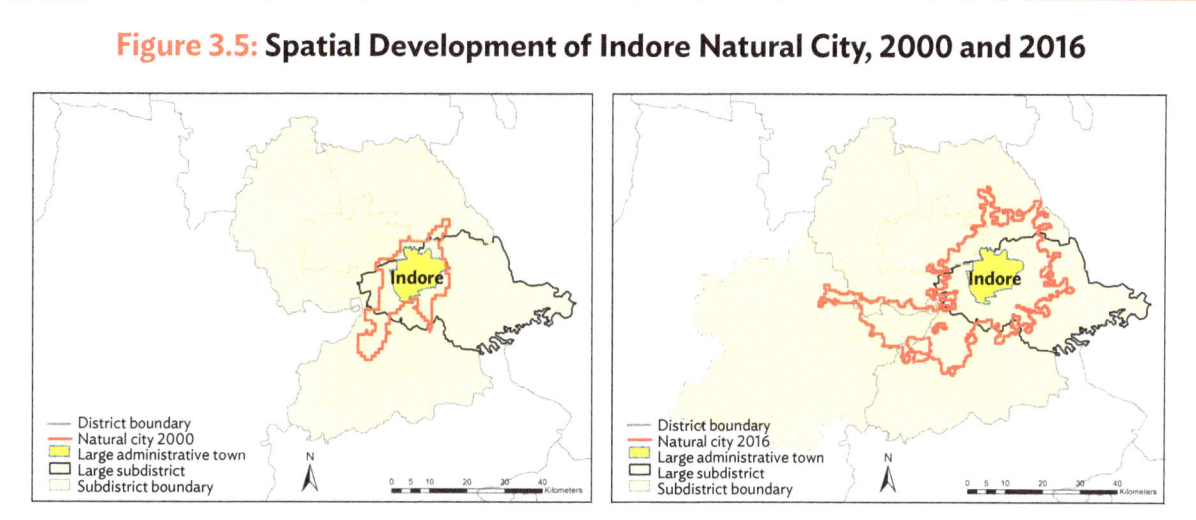

Figure 3.5: Spatial Development of Indore Natural City, 2000 and 2016

Notes: India administrative boundaries are digitized from physical maps and conform to data from the population census of 2011. Boundaries are shown for selected large administrative towns and subdistricts for expositional purposes.
Sources: ADB estimates using (i) nighttime lights images from the National Oceanic and Atmospheric Administration https://ngdc.noaa.gov/eog/ (accessed 1 April 2017 and 10 August 2018 and since 2019 available from the Colorado School of Mines); and (ii) India administrative shapefiles from World Bank Spatial Database for South Asia. www.worldbank.org/spatialdatabase-southasia (accessed 7 September 2016).

---

[36] Economic Census estimates for Indore AC cover the subdistricts of Hatod and Indore.

Indore's economic activity is led by manufacturing in the NC and services in the AC.[37] The expansion of Indore NC's spatial footprint has resulted from relocation and development of formal and large-scale manufacturing activities outside the AC. In 2013, Indore AC had almost 310,000 workers in manufacturing and services (excluding public administration and defense),[38] while the NC had a little less than 436,000 people employed, i.e., about 41% more than Indore AC. Indore NC's share of employment in manufacturing was 28.5% versus 23.1% for the AC. Moreover, there were many more large enterprises in the NC than in the AC.

Connectivity and the existing base of the industrial ecosystem were the key to Indore NC's manufacturing competitiveness vis-à-vis its AC.[39] Dewas, Mhow Cantt, and Pitthampur towns are about 30 kilometers from Indore AC. Also, the prime large-scale industrial clusters in the NC are along AB road, which is part of the Delhi–Mumbai Industrial Corridor.

Analysis of data from the Economic Census 2013–14 indicates that manufacturing of motor vehicles and various electrical machinery and apparatuses was important in the NC and outside Indore AC. Further, the Indore–Dewas region had a high concentration of agro-processing and textile industries. Indore city is close to the Pithampur industrial area, a major manufacturing base for heavy engineering, automobile manufacturing, pharmaceuticals, and metal works. It also has an ancillary base comprising micro, small, and medium-sized enterprises (MSMEs). Such industries are likely to be associated with future economic dynamism, and nurturing the ecosystem in the NC is probably of great importance.

As India's "cleanest city," Indore could be the service sector hub and the economic growth driver of central India. This will entail consolidated economic and allied urban planning by all the agencies involved in the development of the city.

Machilipatnam

Brief Demographic Profile

Machilipatnam is a coastal town in the state of Andhra Pradesh and had a population of 169,892 according to the 2011 Census of India and a literacy rate of 82.4% (with a male literacy rate of 85.7% and female literacy rate of 79.3%).

Economic Profile and Spatial Growth

The employment structure of Machilipatnam AC is dominated by the tertiary sector (about 48.1%), followed by the secondary (27.2%) and primary (24.7%) sectors.[40] Overall, the important subsectors are trade and transport, which have the highest share of employment (24.8%) followed by manufacturing (24.5%) and professional and business services[41] and agriculture (20.7%).

---

[37] The Economic Census 2013–14 estimates for Indore NC cover six subdistricts as against only two subdistricts for Indore AC.
[38] "Services" includes electricity, gas, and water supply, as well as construction, although these subsectors are usually classified as "industries."
[39] Information based on stakeholder consultations held by the study team from 29 November 2021 to 3 December 2021 in Madhya Pradesh.
[40] Economic Census estimates for Machilipatnam AC cover the subdistrict of Machilipatnam.
[41] Includes financial intermediation, insurance and pension funding, real estate, other business activities, and other services auxiliary to financial services.

Key manufacturing industries in the city are food processing, handicrafts (Kalamkari cloth printing), jewelry, leather, and engineering products (auto parts). The Andhra Scientific Company, the major industrial establishment in Machilipatnam, manufactures scientific instruments that are mainly used in laboratories. Bharat Electronics Ltd. is the major electronics manufacturer in the city.

Figure 3.6 depicts the Machilipatnam AC, much of the district of Machilipatnam, and parts of adjoining districts. The area shaded green was the AC as per the 2011 Census of India; the extended area, within the red boundary, was the NC in 2000 (left panel) and 2016 (right panel). The NC grew 206.3% from 2000 to 2016. By 2016, the NC area was substantially larger than the AC and the NC population was growing by an average of 2.9% annually. Figure 3.6 illustrates how the NC has evolved spatially since 2000. The NC expanded beyond the AC, mostly to the northeast and southwest. In 2016, the NC spanned one town and 53 villages in Krishna district.

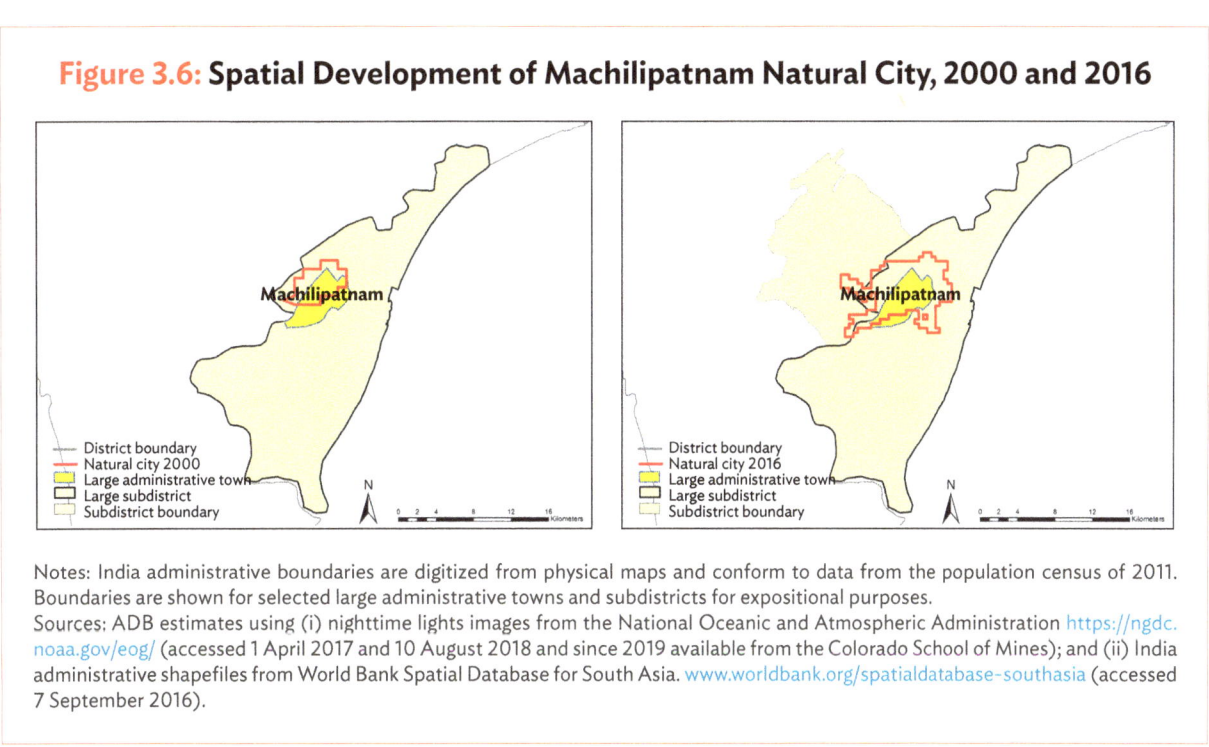

Figure 3.6: Spatial Development of Machilipatnam Natural City, 2000 and 2016

Notes: India administrative boundaries are digitized from physical maps and conform to data from the population census of 2011. Boundaries are shown for selected large administrative towns and subdistricts for expositional purposes.
Sources: ADB estimates using (i) nighttime lights images from the National Oceanic and Atmospheric Administration https://ngdc.noaa.gov/eog/ (accessed 1 April 2017 and 10 August 2018 and since 2019 available from the Colorado School of Mines); and (ii) India administrative shapefiles from World Bank Spatial Database for South Asia. www.worldbank.org/spatialdatabase-southasia (accessed 7 September 2016).

Economic growth has been led by manufacturing beyond the AC. The NC's spatial footprint reflects relocation and development of manufacturing activities outside the AC.[42] In 2013, the AC had almost 27,000 workers in manufacturing and services (excluding public administration and defense) while the NC had a little over 33,000, i.e., about 23.9% more than the AC. The share of employment in manufacturing was higher in the NC (26.6%) than in the AC (24.5%).

Machilipatnam has to find its own identity capitalizing on its access to the sea. The state could usefully undertake an exercise to determine how the city could position itself and which sectors could lead to further development.

---

[42] The Economic Census estimates for Machilipatnam NC cover two subdistricts versus only one subdistrict for the AC.

Nalgonda

Brief Demographic Profile

Nalgonda city is close to the Telangana state capital of Hyderabad. Nalgonda had 154,326 people as per the 2011 Census of India and a literacy rate of 86.8% (with a male literacy rate of 92.9% and female literacy rate of 80.8%).

Economic Profile and Spatial Growth

Nalgonda district contributed 6.6% (about ₹4.5 billion—about $72 million) of Telangana state's economy in 2014–2015. In terms of the sectoral composition of employment, the AC's tertiary sector accounted for about 70.6%, followed by the secondary (23.0%) and primary (6.5%) sectors.[43] Within the tertiary sector, trade had the highest share (27.0%) followed by professional and business services (17.8%). Key manufacturing subsectors by share of establishments and employment included food processing (fruit, seeds, and rice processing, and dairy products); machinery (iron, steel, and quartz-based products); and chemical manufacturing (adhesives, lubricants, and pharmaceutical formulation ingredients) industries.

Figure 3.7 depicts Nalgonda AC, much of the district of Nalgonda, and parts of adjoining districts. The area shaded green was the AC as per the 2011 Census of India; the extended area, within the red boundary, was the NC in 2000 (left panel) and 2016 (right panel). The NC of Nalgonda grew 211.9% from 2000 to 2016 and, by 2016, was substantially larger than the AC. During the same period, the NC

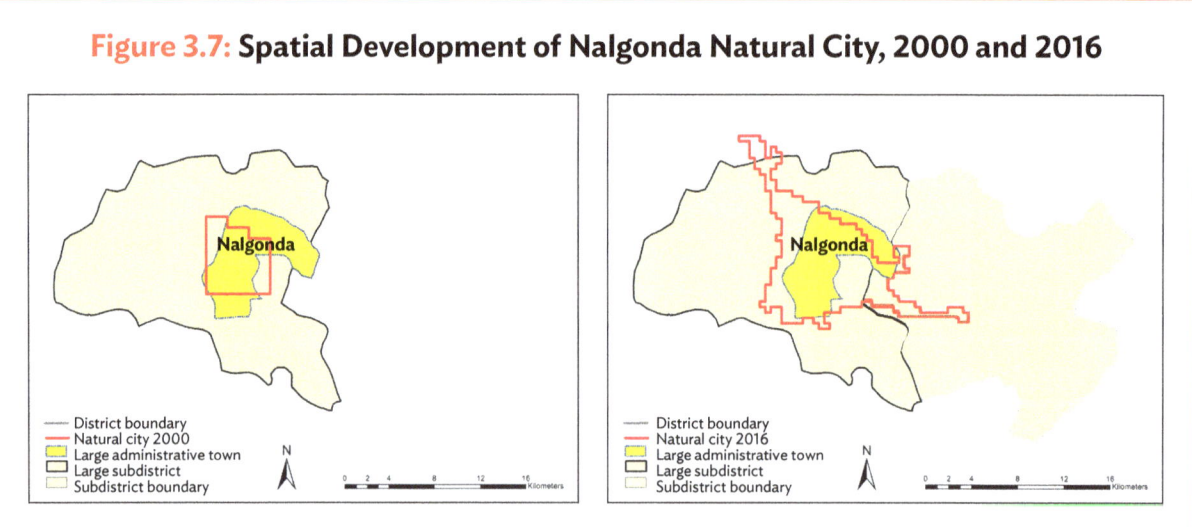

Figure 3.7: Spatial Development of Nalgonda Natural City, 2000 and 2016

Notes: India administrative boundaries are digitized from physical maps and conform to data from the population census of 2011. Boundaries are shown for selected large administrative towns and subdistricts for expositional purposes.
Sources: ADB estimates using (i) nighttime lights images from the National Oceanic and Atmospheric Administration https://ngdc.noaa.gov/eog/ (accessed 1 April 2017 and 10 August 2018 and since 2019 available from the Colorado School of Mines); and (ii) India administrative shapefiles from World Bank Spatial Database for South Asia. www.worldbank.org/spatialdatabase-southasia (accessed 7 September 2016).

---

[43] Economic Census estimates for Nalgonda AC cover the Nalgonda subdistrict.

population grew an average of 2.8% annually. Figure 3.7 illustrates the change since 2000. The NC spread beyond the AC, primarily to the northwest and southeast. In 2016, the NC spanned one town and 43 villages in Nalgonda district.

Navsari

Brief Demographic Profile

Navsari is close to the historically significant beach of Dandi, and is a coastal town in the state of Gujarat. Navsari had 171,109 people according to the 2011 Census of India and a literacy rate of 88.4% (with a male literacy rate of 92.0% and female literacy rate of 84.4%).

Economic Profile and Spatial Growth

Manufacturing is driving the economic growth of Navsari AC.[44] The secondary sector accounts for a major share (58.1%) of the employment in the city, followed by the tertiary (36.1%) and primary (5.8%) sectors. Key manufacturing subsectors in Navsari include furniture, agro-industry and food processing (sugar, mango pulp, and refined oil); textiles (power loom, grey cloth processing, and yarn crimping and weaving); chemical and chemical-based products (drugs and pharmaceuticals); rubber- and plastic-based products (PVC pipes and cable and electrical accessories); and engineering products (agricultural equipment, rolling shutters, and tin containers). Navsari city has an industrial legacy in textiles and diamond processing, and the district of Navsari (a coastal district) has access to a strong base of fishing industries.

The urban footprint of Navsari NC has changed considerably since 2000. Figure 3.8 (right side) depicts Navsari AC, much of the district of Navsari, and parts of adjoining districts. The area shaded green was the AC as per the 2011 Census of India, and the extended area, within the red boundary, was the NC in 2000 (left panel) and 2016 (right panel). The NC expanded significantly from 2000 to 2016, growing in area by 118.8%. By 2016, the NC area was substantially larger than its administrative counterpart. The NC had spread beyond the administrative borders, primarily to the south and southeast. In 2016, the NC of Navsari spanned four towns and 65 villages in Navsari district.

Navsari's economic growth has been led by manufacturing within the AC; however, since 1990, a majority of the industrial units within the AC have closed or relocated outside it. The increased spatial footprint of the NC has resulted from development of formal and large-scale manufacturing activities within the administrative boundary only. Because the Navsari NC and AC comprise one and the same subdistrict (Navsari subdistrict), estimates of employment from the Economic Census 2013–14 are the same for both. In 2013, about 72,800 workers were in manufacturing and services (excluding public administration and defense).[45]

---

[44] Economic Census estimates for Navsari AC cover the subdistrict of Navsari.
[45] "Services" includes electricity, gas, and water supply as well as construction although these subsectors are usually classified as "industries."

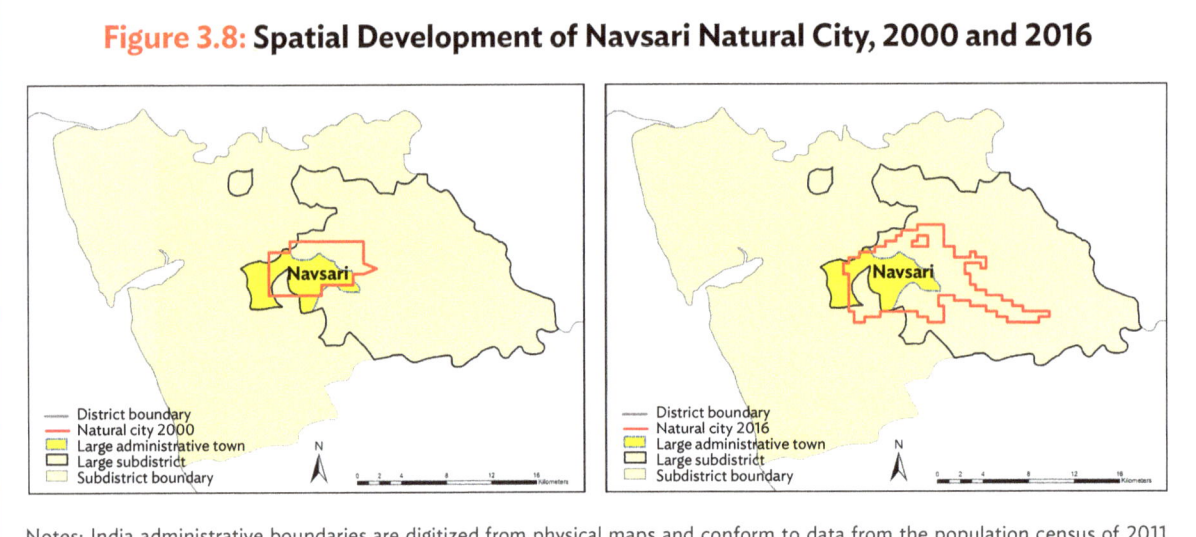

Figure 3.8: **Spatial Development of Navsari Natural City, 2000 and 2016**

Notes: India administrative boundaries are digitized from physical maps and conform to data from the population census of 2011. Boundaries are shown for selected large administrative towns and subdistricts for expositional purposes.
Sources: ADB estimates using (i) nighttime lights images from the National Oceanic and Atmospheric Administration https://ngdc.noaa.gov/eog/ (accessed 1 April 2017 and 10 August 2018 and since 2019 available from the Colorado School of Mines); and (ii) India administrative shapefiles from World Bank Spatial Database for South Asia. www.worldbank.org/spatialdatabase-southasia (accessed 7 September 2016).

Since the 1990s, a majority of industrial enterprises have either closed or moved out of the Navsari AC. Some key examples include the Navsari Cotton Mills and Mafatlal Industries. Also, all the local diamond polishing and processing centers have closed. Some of the prominent industries have relocated toward the National Highway, with a significant number of manufacturing industries on the south and eastern sides (along the Navsari–Surat highway, the Navsari–Gandevi road, etc.).

Under the new master plan 2029, the city limits have been significantly increased. This will enable new planned development beyond the current congested city.

Navsari has to completely reinvent itself on account of economic decline and migration of youth and working population to other cities and countries. To stop this drain, it is imperative that the city charts a new development trajectory based on its natural conditions and focusing on improving urban infrastructure and services.

Sonipat

Brief Demographic Profile

Sonipat is in the National Capital Region. Sonipat city had a population of 289,333 as per the 2011 Census of India and a literacy rate of 85.5% (with a male literacy rate of 90.8% and female literacy rate of 79.4%).

Economic Profile

Sonipat's economy largely depends on the secondary sector. According to the Economic Census 2013–14, the secondary sector accounted for 41.9% of the AC's employment.[46] The primary sector contributed about 9.8% and the tertiary sector about 48.2%. Key manufacturing subsectors in the city are food products; automotive (parts and components of motor vehicles and trailers and semi-trailers); basic metal manufacturing; and manufacturing of medical, precision, and optical instruments as well as watches and clocks.

Figure 3.9 depicts the Sonipat AC according to the 2011 Census of India and adjacent or nearby towns and villages. Because the Sonipat AC is within Delhi's NC, it is not possible to define an independent Sonipat NC. In 2013, Sonipat AC had almost 104,000 workers in manufacturing and services industries (excluding public administration and defense).

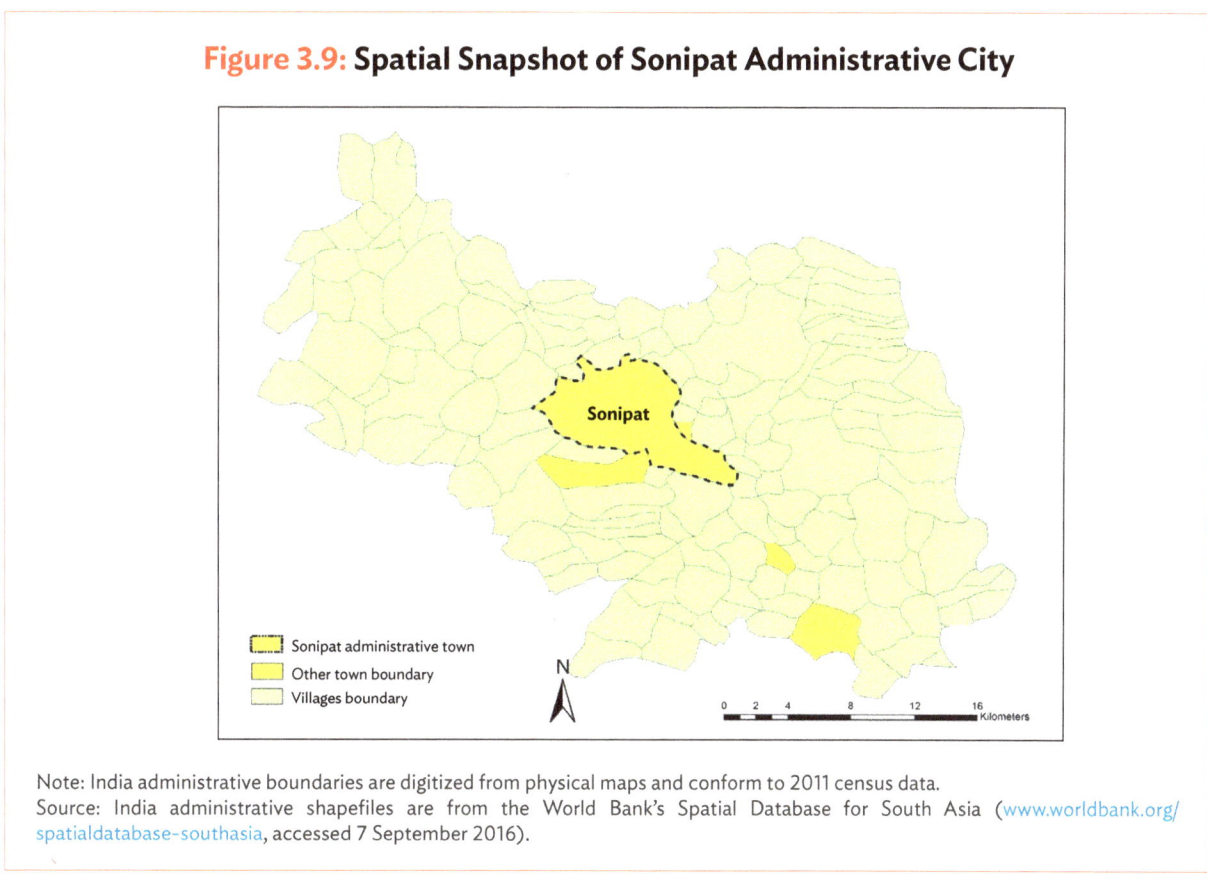

Figure 3.9: Spatial Snapshot of Sonipat Administrative City

Note: India administrative boundaries are digitized from physical maps and conform to 2011 census data.
Source: India administrative shapefiles are from the World Bank's Spatial Database for South Asia (www.worldbank.org/spatialdatabase-southasia, accessed 7 September 2016).

Sonipat's economic growth is contingent on how it can capitalize on the proximity with Delhi and other parts of the National Capital Region. Sonipat's key advantages include the availability of land for service and manufacturing subsectors and its proximity to Delhi. The key to unlocking the city's potential is urban infrastructure and services, which could attract high-skilled manpower to shift to the city.

---

[46] Economic Census estimates for Sonipat AC cover the subdistrict of Sonipat.

Vadodara

Brief Demographic Profile

Vadodara is the third largest city in the state of Gujarat. The city had a population of 1,752,371 as per the 2011 Census of India and a literacy rate of 90.6% (with a male literacy rate of 93.8% and female literacy rate of 87.2%).

Economic Profile and Spatial Growth

Vadodara AC contributes more than half of Vadodara district's economy.[47] The employment structure in the AC was 61.2% in tertiary, 35.1% in secondary, and 3.7% in primary sectors.[48] Within the tertiary sector, the largest shares of employment were in trade (30.2%) and professional and business services (18.1%).[49] Key manufacturing subsectors in Vadodara by share of establishments and employment included chemicals (fertilizers, insecticides, and pharmaceutical products); machinery (power transmission and distribution equipment); and fabricated metal products (fittings, fasteners, and pipes).

Vadodara has traditionally been home to chemicals companies. Production of dolomite and fluorspar is an important activity—Vadodara has accounted for as much as 98% of Gujarat's total production of dolomite (IBEF 2021). Vadodara city is an emerging automotive hub. The presence of auto makers in the district has also contributed to the rise of MSMEs in and around Vadodara.

The urban footprint of Vadodara NC has evolved considerably since 2000. Figure 3.10 (right side) depicts the city of Vadodara including the AC, much of the district of Vadodara, and parts of adjoining districts. The area shaded green was Vadodara AC as per the 2011 Census of India and the extended area, within the red boundary, was the NC in 2000 (left panel) and 2016 (right panel). Vadodara's NC area grew considerably from 2000 to 2016, by 104.3%. By 2016, the NC area was substantially larger than its administrative counterpart. From 2000 to 2016, the NC population grew an average 2.0% annually. The NC's area reached beyond the AC borders, primarily to the north, northwest, and west. In 2016, the NC spanned 19 towns and 543 villages in 2 districts (Anand and Vadodara).

Economic growth had been led by manufacturing outside Vadodara AC, but traditional industries are still concentrated in the AC. The growing footprint of the NC has included relocation and development of formal and large-scale manufacturing activities outside the administrative boundary.[50] In 2013, the Vadodara AC had almost 325,000 workers in manufacturing and services[51] (excluding public administration and defense) while the NC had a little over 415,000 people employed: about 27.7% more than the Vadodara AC.

---

[47] Information collected based on stakeholder consultations.
[48] Economic Census estimates for Vadodara AC cover the subdistrict of Vadodara.
[49] Includes financial intermediation, insurance, and pension funding; real estate; other business activities; and other services auxiliary to financial services.
[50] Economic Census estimates for Vadodara NC cover six subdistricts as against only one subdistrict for Vadodara AC.
[51] "Services" here includes electricity, gas, and water supply as well as construction although these subsectors are usually classified as "industries."

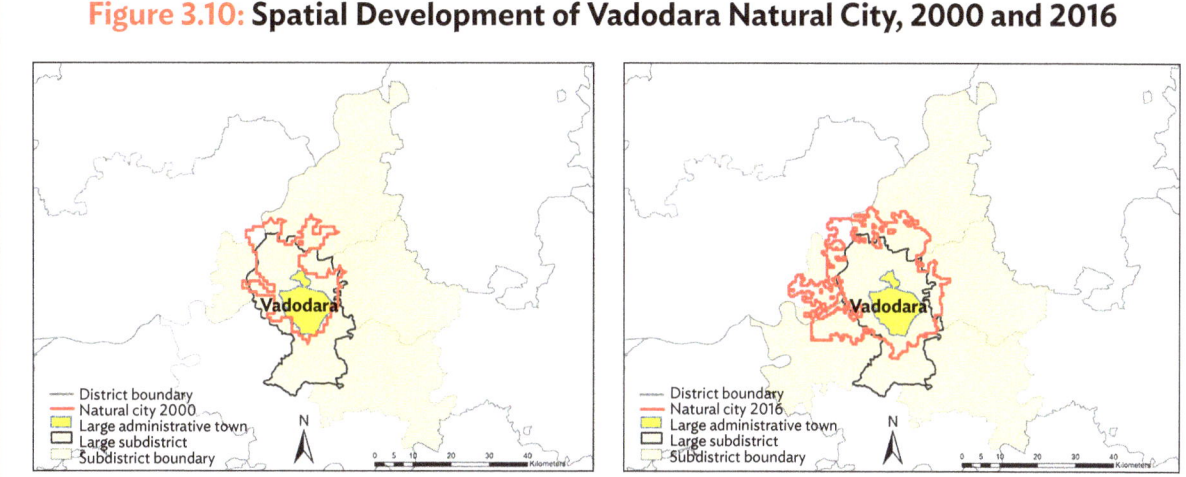

Figure 3.10: **Spatial Development of Vadodara Natural City, 2000 and 2016**

Notes: India administrative boundaries are digitized from physical maps and conform to data from the population census of 2011. Boundaries are shown for selected large administrative towns and subdistricts for expositional purposes.
Sources: ADB estimates using (i) nighttime lights images from the National Oceanic and Atmospheric Administration https://ngdc.noaa.gov/eog/ (accessed 1 April 2017 and 10 August 2018 and since 2019 available from the Colorado School of Mines); and (ii) India administrative shapefiles from World Bank Spatial Database for South Asia. www.worldbank.org/spatialdatabase-southasia (accessed 7 September 2016).

Vadodara NC and AC had almost the same shares of employment in manufacturing (30.1% for the NC versus 30.5% for the AC). However, the NC had 28.9% more manufacturing enterprises than the AC. Approximately 40% of the medium and large-scale industries (such as Gujarat State Fertilizers and Chemicals Ltd., Gujarat Refinery, Indian Petrochemicals Corporation Ltd., and Gujarat Alkalies and Chemicals Ltd.) were within Vadodara AC. Major public and private sector industries in the northwest occupied about 15.2% of the urban area (VUDA 2007).

As one of the key cities in the state of Gujarat, the city has to focus on developing and implementing a comprehensive economic and urban development plan in order to enable service sector industries to move into the city and provide high-quality urban services to residents.

Vijayawada

Brief Demographic Profile

Vijayawada is the second largest city in the state of Andhra Pradesh. The city's population was 1,143,232 as per the 2011 Census of India, and had a literacy rate of 81.2% (with a male literacy rate of 85.0% and female literacy rate of 77.5%).

Economic Profile and Spatial Growth

The economy of Vijayawada largely depends on the tertiary sector. According to the Economic Census 2013–14, the tertiary sector accounted for 76.7% of the AC's employment, followed by the secondary (21.7%) and primary (1.6%) sectors.[52] Within the tertiary sector, trade had the highest share (43%), followed by transport (9%) and professional and business services (9%).[53] Key manufacturing subsectors in Vijayawada by share of establishments and employment included heavy machinery, food processing, and chemical manufacturing industries. The first industries set up in the city were for food processing, such as for rice, pulses, and oil seeds. These industries began growing in Vijayawada because of its good connections with important marketing and consumption centers in the region.

The development in 1966 of Jawahar Auto Nagar Industrial Estate, in the eastern part of the city near Patamata and covering about 111 hectares (275 acres), led to the emergence of a number of ancillary industrial units (IBEF 2021).

Figure 3.11 depicts Vijayawada AC, much of the district of Vijayawada, and parts of adjoining districts. The area shaded green was the AC as per the 2011 Census of India and the extended area, within the red boundary, was the NC in 2000 (left panel) and 2016 (right panel). The NC of Vijayawada grew 240.1% from 2000 to 2016 while its population grew by an average of 1.5% annually. The NC's area extended beyond the AC borders, primarily to the northwest, northeast, and southwest. In 2016, the NC spanned 14 towns and 275 villages in 3 districts (Guntur, Krishna, and West Godavari).

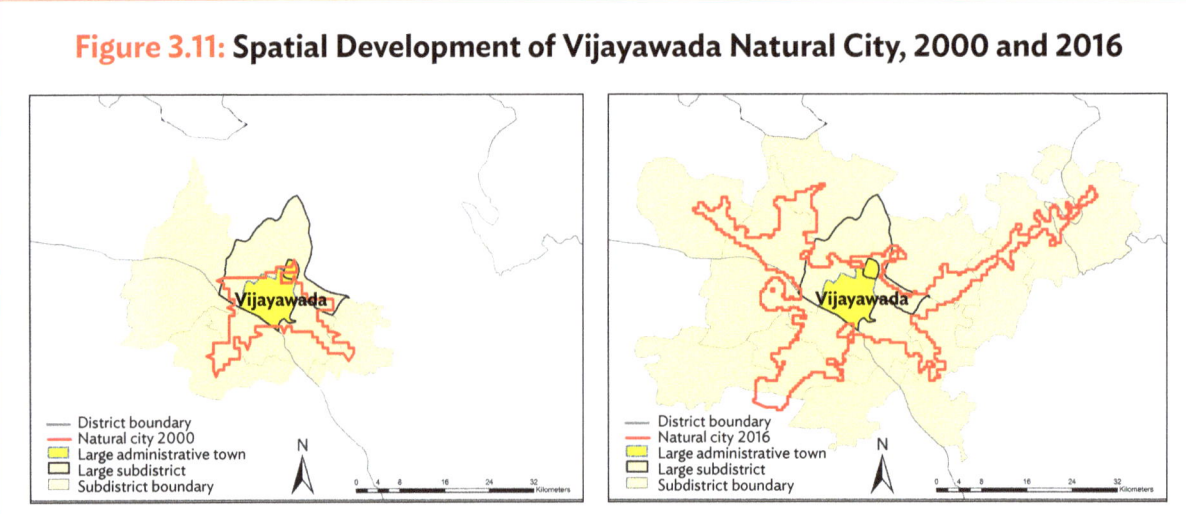

Figure 3.11: Spatial Development of Vijayawada Natural City, 2000 and 2016

Notes: India administrative boundaries are digitized from physical maps and conform to data from the population census of 2011. Boundaries are shown for selected large administrative towns and subdistricts for expositional purposes.
Sources: ADB estimates using (i) nighttime lights images from the National Oceanic and Atmospheric Administration https://ngdc.noaa.gov/eog/ (accessed 1 April 2017 and 10 August 2018 and since 2019 available from the Colorado School of Mines); and (ii) India administrative shapefiles from World Bank Spatial Database for South Asia www.worldbank.org/spatialdatabase-southasia (accessed 7 September 2016).

---

[52] Economic Census estimates for Vijayawada AC cover the subdistricts of Vijayawada (rural), Vijayawada (urban), and Penamaluru.
[53] Includes financial intermediation, insurance and pension funding, real estate, other business activities, and other services auxiliary to financial services.

Economic growth has been led by manufacturing beyond the AC and services within it. The increased spatial footprint of the NC has resulted from relocation and development of formal and large-scale manufacturing activities outside the AC.[54] In 2013, the AC had almost 291,000 workers in manufacturing and services (excluding public administration and defense) while the NC had almost 443,000—52.4% more than the AC.[55] However, The NC had a slightly lower share of employment in manufacturing (17.7%) than the AC (17.9%). The NC had many more large enterprises than the AC (412 against 331).

Warangal

Brief Demographic Profile

Warangal is the second largest city in the state of Telangana. The city had 704,570 people as per the 2011 Census of India and a literacy rate of 83.3% (with a male literacy rate of 90.4% and female literacy rate of 76.2%).

Economic Profile and Spatial Growth

Warangal AC's tertiary sector accounted for 67.4% of the city's employment, followed by the secondary (28.1%) and primary (4.5%) sectors.[56] Within the tertiary sector, trade had the highest share at 31% followed by social subsectors such as education, health, and hotels. Key manufacturing subsectors in Warangal by share of establishments and employment include food processing, textiles and apparel, furniture, machinery, and nonmetallic mineral products.

The Warangal urban district has 1,366 MSMEs, which were established with a total investment of $60.3 million and provide direct employment to more than 5,800 people (Mahender 2021). The urban district has just five large or medium enterprises (whose activities include producing rice bran oil, cotton seed oil, dairy products, and solar power) with an investment of $22.4 million, providing direct employment to 427 people.

Warangal NC has expanded since 2000. Figure 3.12 depicts Warangal AC, much of the district of Warangal, and parts of adjoining districts. The area shaded green was the AC as per the 2011 Census of India and the extended area, within the red boundary, was the NC in 2000 (left panel) and 2016 (right panel). From 2000 to 2016, the NC grew 62.3%, and by 2016 was substantially larger than the AC. From 2000 to 2016, the NC population grew an average of 1.5% annually. Figure 3.12 illustrates how the NC has evolved since 2000. The NC's area reached beyond the AC borders, primarily to the northeast and southwest. In 2016, the NC spanned 6 towns and 93 villages in Warangal district.

---

[54] Economic Census estimates for Vijayawada NC cover 17 subdistricts as against only three subdistricts covered under Vijayawada AC.
[55] "Services" includes electricity, gas, and water supply as well as construction although these subsectors are usually classified as "industries."
[56] Economic Census estimates for Warangal AC cover the subdistricts of Dharmasagar, Geesugonda, Hanamkonda, Hasanparthy, and Warangal.

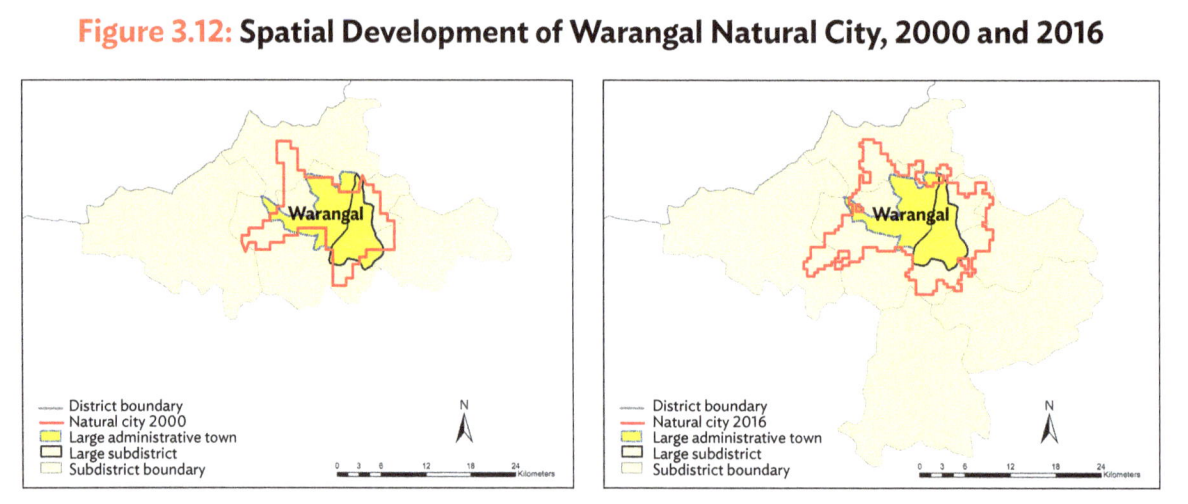

Figure 3.12: **Spatial Development of Warangal Natural City, 2000 and 2016**

Notes: India administrative boundaries are digitized from physical maps and conform to data from the population census of 2011. Boundaries are shown for selected large administrative towns and subdistricts for expositional purposes.
Sources: ADB estimates using (i) nighttime lights images from the National Oceanic and Atmospheric Administration https://ngdc.noaa.gov/eog/ (accessed 1 April 2017 and 10 August 2018 and since 2019 available from the Colorado School of Mines); and (ii) India administrative shapefiles from World Bank Spatial Database for South Asia. www.worldbank.org/spatialdatabase-southasia (accessed 7 September 2016).

In 2013, the AC had more than 113,000 workers in manufacturing and services industries (excluding public administration and defense)[57] while the NC had more than 121,000—about 7.2% more than the AC. Warangal NC had a slightly lower share of employment in manufacturing (24.0%) than the AC (24.2%).[58] The NC had 35 large enterprises (employing 100 or more people), which was only one more than that in the AC.

Warangal has a lot of positive factors (low cost of living, proximity to Hyderabad, availability of institutes for higher and technical education, etc.) that, if capitalized upon, could drive Warangal as a focal point for the service sector, especially in information technology and information-technology-enabled services. Such service industries could be attracted to the city if it provides high-quality urban services and a real estate market catering to retail, hospitality, education, and healthcare.

Summary

Cities have expanded well beyond their administrative boundaries. By 2016, most of the NCs examined had a significant portion of their area lying outside the 2011 boundaries of their corresponding ACs. The expansion of NCs has meant that each covers multiple administrative units. For example, in 2016, Indore NC spanned 28 towns and 1,074 villages in two districts while Guwahati NC spanned 27 towns and 1,114 villages in four districts. Without a mechanism to coordinate economic and spatial planning across multiple administrative units, urbanization has likely proceeded in a haphazard manner and the full benefits from agglomeration economies are not being realized. The stakeholder consultations that are described next suggest this has been the case.

---

[57] "Services" includes electricity, gas, and water supply as well as construction although these are usually classified as "industries."
[58] Economic Census estimates for Warangal NC cover seven subdistricts and only five subdistricts for Warangal AC.

References

Asian Development Bank (ADB). 2019. *Asian Development Outlook 2019 Update: Fostering Growth and Inclusion in Asia's Cities.*

———. Natural Cities Database. Unpublished.

Directorate of Economics and Statistics (DES), Madhya Pradesh. n.d. Economic Survey of Madhya Pradesh 2017–18 (Hindi). http://14.139.60.153/bitstream/123456789/13019/1/Economic%20Survey%20of%20madhya%20pradesh%202017-18.pdf.

Indian Brand Equity Foundation (IBEF). 2021. Gujarat. PowerPoint presentation. https://www.ibef.org/download/Gujarat-June-2021.pdf

Mahender, A. 2021. Industrial Growth: Warangal Awaits a Giant Leap. *The Hans India*. 18 February 2021. https://www.thehansindia.com/business/industrial-growth-warangal-awaits-a-giant-leap-672823 (accessed February 2022).

Ministry of Micro, Small and Medium Enterprises (MMSME), Government of India. n.d. Brief Industrial Profile of Dewas District, Madhya Pradesh. n.d. (date likely 2012). http://dcmsme.gov.in/old/dips/frorma%20-%20dips%20-%20Dewas%20(2).pdf (accessed February 2022).

Ministry of Statistics and Programme Implementation (MOSPI), Government of India. 2018a. *India—Fourth Economic Census 1998*. National Data Archive. http://microdata.gov.in/nada43/index.php/catalog/56.

———. 2018b. *India—Sixth Economic Census 2013–14*. National Data Archive. http://microdata.gov.in/nada43/index.php/catalog/47.

———. MOSPI Database. n.d. http://microdata.gov.in/nada43/index.php/catalog/ECO (accessed January–March 2022).

National Oceanic and Atmospheric Administration (NOAA). https://ngdc.noaa.gov/eog/ (accessed 1 April 2017 and 10 August 2018). Nighttime light data are available since 2019 from the Colorado School of Mines.

Office of the Registrar General and Census Commissioner, India (ORGCC). n.d. Census 1998. https://censusindia.gov.in/census.website/ (accessed January–March 2022).

———. n.d. 2011 Census of India. https://censusindia.gov.in/census.website/ (accessed January–March 2022).

Vadodara Urban Development Authority (VUDA). 2007. Second Revised Draft Development Plan 2031—Vadodara. VUDA. November 2007.

World Bank. 2016. Spatial Database for South Asia. www.worldbank.org/spatialdatabase-southasia (accessed 7 September 2016)

Chapter 4

Stakeholder Consultations to Identify Growth Bottlenecks

With the understanding of the economic and spatial profile of the shortlisted cities gained from the analysis of the previous chapters, an inception workshop was conducted in October 2021 with regional, metropolitan, state, and central government stakeholders and representatives from industry associations. The workshop was held to (i) discuss the rationale and objectives of the study with officials from the project states and cities, (ii) discuss the approach proposed to meet the objectives of the study, and (iii) request appointments with the stakeholders in government and the private sector for gathering data and insights. The workshop also described the global best practices in city-led economic growth and provided an opportunity for government stakeholders to share their experiences in this area.

Participants at the workshop welcomed the study and noted that a better understanding of the economics of cities and how their full economic potential could be harnessed was needed. Highlights of points made by the officials included the following:

- Confirmation of Chapter 3's findings that the economics of a city extended well beyond its municipal boundaries and that the process of relocating manufacturing to the periphery of cities was under way.

- The economics of cities, defined broadly, was driven by both manufacturing and services and thus analysis must consider both.

- Economically dynamic cities in India were attractive to investors and entrepreneurs not so much due to "subsidies" offered to business, but because they provided a good ecosystem for conducting business.

- Good coordination between the various departments, including between the industry and urban departments, was essential.[59]

- More generally, gaps in interdepartmental coordination and inconsistencies in regulatory frameworks needed to be identified and tackled.

---

[59] For example, different interpretations of industrial plots/building codes by two or more departments can delay investments and economic activity.

◯ States and cities must assess how master plans, land-use plans, town development schemes, and models for aggregating land can be improved given their effect on the economic dynamism of cities.[60]

◯ Urban local bodies must play a bigger role in making cities an engine of growth and generating employment opportunities.

◯ Cities and states need differentiated strategies that factor in their comparative advantages and geographical realities. Too many cities adopting the same strategy could be counterproductive.

Subsequent to the workshop, more than 100 stakeholders in the government and private sectors were identified for evaluating the key issues constraining the cities from fully realizing their economic potential. The study team held discussions with stakeholders from the seven states and the 12 shortlisted cities from November 2021 through February 2022 (Figure 4.1).

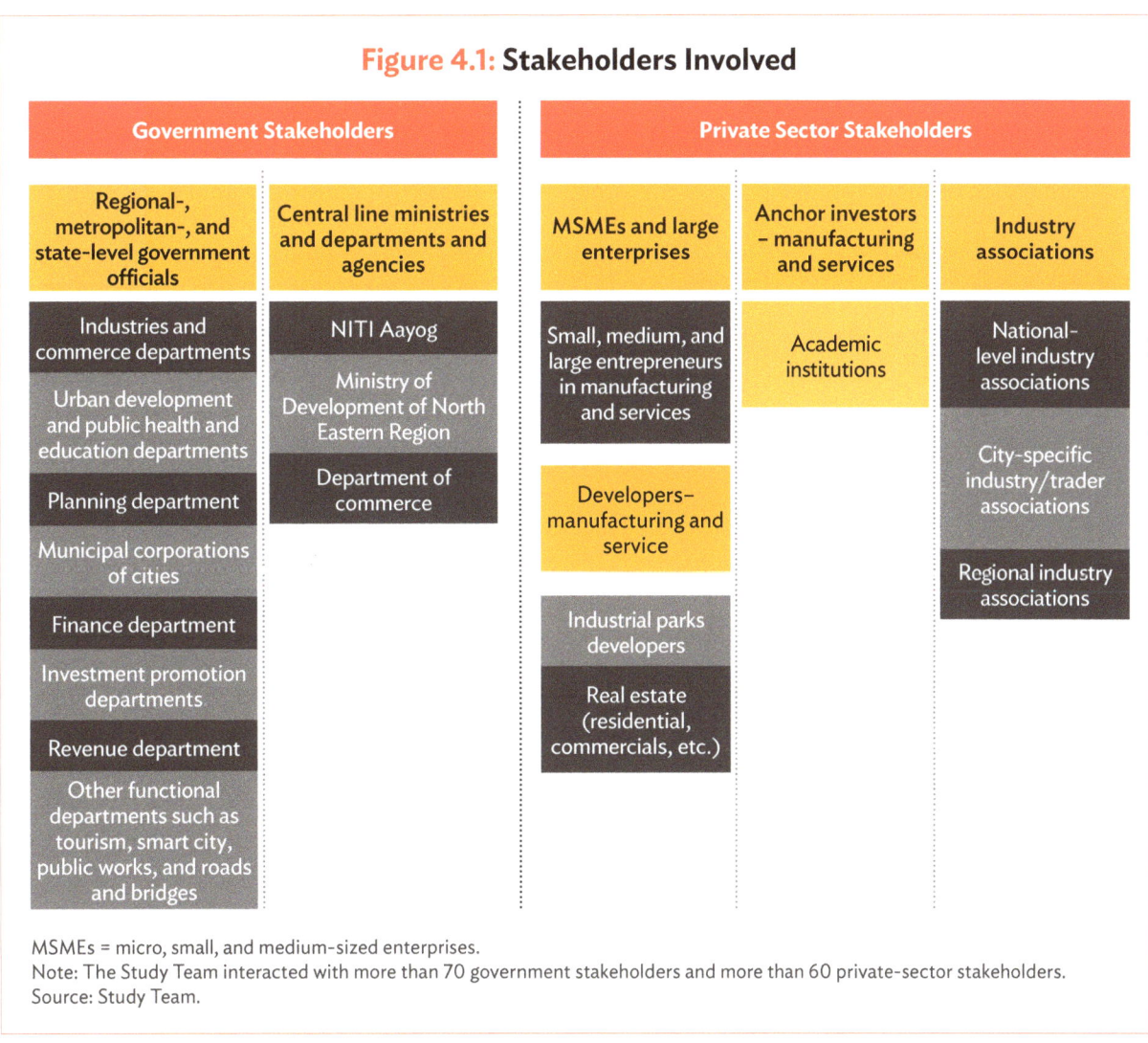

Figure 4.1: Stakeholders Involved

MSMEs = micro, small, and medium-sized enterprises.
Note: The Study Team interacted with more than 70 government stakeholders and more than 60 private-sector stakeholders.
Source: Study Team.

---

[60] For example, participants noted that effective master plans should be based on anticipating investor needs.

The team identified and carried out interviews with stakeholders on two levels.

⊃ **Supply-side considerations.** The study team held discussions with government officials to understand the broader economic–spatial relations, urban and peri-urban dynamics, and the factors driving economic growth in prioritized states and cities. Departments at the regional, metropolitan, and state levels included municipal corporations, industries and commerce, urban planning, investment promotion, finance, regional development authorities, revenue, apex bodies such as the North Eastern Council, and others. The central line agencies consulted included the Ministry of Development of North Eastern Region. Table 4.1 summarizes the structured interview themes prepared for consultations with government stakeholders.

Table 4.1: Key Structured Interview Themes for Government Stakeholders

General Area of Investigation	Specific Queries/Discussion Areas
What are the Supply-Side Enablers of Economic Growth?	• How are master plans spatially directing investments? • What infrastructure is being provided in order to attract growth or investment? • What legal frameworks are in place to support investment initiatives (such as the Special Investment Regions Act)?
Key Clusters, Areas, and Hubs of the City	• Spatial analysis of identified key subsectors (clusters, industrial parks, etc.) • Percent of industrial land use in natural city and suburb areas • Analysis of registration data of micro, small, and medium-sized enterprises and service sector firms in the last 10 years for the natural city or the municipal limits
Master Plan (and regional plan if applicable) and Supporting Infrastructure	• Regional integration • Trends in prioritizing industrial growth: analysis of current vs. the previous master plan • Current master plan growth corridors vs. actual city expansion • Gaps: vision vs. reality • Trunk infrastructure provisions • Access to social infrastructure
Policies and Investments	• Laws, acts, and regulations governing industrial development—licenses, permits, approvals, judicial systems, taxes, etc. • Local schemes/policies for industrial, manufacturing, and services • Short-term investment decisions/plans

Source: Study Team.

⊃ **Demand-side considerations.** To better understand the present environment for doing business in the region, the study team held discussions with private sector actors including investors; developers; industry associations; and small, medium, and large enterprises. This included understanding their opinions about the physical, social, infrastructure, and economic parameters that they considered when deciding whether to set up and/or expand their facilities and the key interventions they would expect the government to provide to improve the business climate.

The private sector representatives (developers and investors) were from micro, small, and medium-sized enterprises as well as large enterprises. The consultations included industry associations, such as the Confederation of Indian Industry, Federation of Indian Chambers of Commerce and Industry,

Indian Chamber of Commerce, PHD Chamber of Commerce and Industry, and Federation of Industry and Commerce of North Eastern Region. Academic institutions included the Indian Institute of Management and Indore and Sikkim Manipal University. Table 4.2 lists the structured interview themes for consultations with private sector stakeholders.

Table 4.2: Key Structured Interview Themes for Private Sector Stakeholders

Investor Category	Queries Posed
Existing Investors in the City/Region	• Key drivers for investment: ■ Policies and incentives ■ Ease of doing business (EODB) initiatives ■ Infrastructure ■ Suppliers, raw material base ■ Historical base ■ Skill availability • What are your opinions about enabling areas of industrial investments? ■ Policies and incentives ■ EODB initiatives ■ Infrastructure availability ■ Supplier and raw material base ■ Historical industry base ■ Skill availability • What are your key plans for future expansion in the city? • Do you have plans to expand in any other city? • What key areas of interventions are required from the government for you to expand?
Investors that Left the City/Region	• What were the key reasons for you to shift your base out of the city? ■ Infrastructure ■ Hurdles in EODB ■ Supplier/raw material base ■ Skill availability ■ Regulatory environment ■ Better opportunity in other location • What key areas of intervention could have been taken to ensure that you would not have left?
Investors that Considered Investing in the City, But Did Not	• What are the key reasons for you to consider the city as a base? ■ Policies and incentives ■ EODB measures ■ Infrastructure ■ Suppliers, raw material base ■ Skill availability • What are the key areas of interventions by the government needed to ensure you would invest in the city? ■ Infrastructure ■ Logistics ■ Fiscal incentives ■ Skill availability
Industry Associations	• What enables industries to stay or invest in the city? • What are the key areas of government intervention needed? • How is the industry collaborating with the government to improve the industrial ecosystem?

Source: Study Team.

The interviews were subsequently complemented with data from primary sources, including official documents, and with secondary sources such as economic databases and various reports. The economic databases used for the study include those of the Directorate General of Commercial Intelligence and Statistics, International Trade Centre Trade Map, and Intelligence Statistics.

Official documents were collected from the websites of regional, metropolitan, and state government agencies, including gazette notifications; official press statements; industrial information systems; publications such as state and city vision, regional plan, and master plan documents; economic censuses and surveys; the Annual Survey of Industries, 2017–2018; the Reserve Bank of India's *Handbook of Statistics on the Indian Economy*; industrial and investment policies of states; and Labour Bureau publications.

Chapter 5

Key Bottlenecks Constraining the Potential of Cities

As noted in the previous chapter, extensive stakeholder consultations were held to understand in detail how cities could harness their economic potential. A first step was to examine what factors may be holding individual cities back from realizing their potential. Despite the diversity of the cities studied, stakeholders identified many factors common among the cities. The common factors are summarized in Figure 5.1 and then discussed in terms of five broad bottlenecks.

The five broad bottlenecks are (i) a lack of common economic vision; (ii) challenges related to land supply; (iii) master planning that is insufficiently aligned with economic goals, future land use, and infrastructure needs; (iv) inadequate institutional framework and capacity; and (v) business-related policies and regulatory constraints. In general, the bottlenecks are common across all study cities, and very likely reflect the general pattern across most cities throughout India. However, some problem areas tend to be specific to certain cities. For example, locational disadvantages are more relevant for cities in hilly and mountainous areas or where climate patterns combine with topography to make a city more prone to floods or droughts. Of the study cities, Gangtok and Navsari stand out on this challenge. Similarly, the lack of a historical industrial base—due to locations far from major historical transport networks and urban centers of the country—can act as a drag on economic growth, a situation that affects Gangtok and Guwahati to a greater extent than other study cities. Finally, land availability is also affected by geography and even customs: again, Gangtok is an example.

Lack of Common Economic Vision

As Chapter 3 indicates, cities have expanded their economic activities considerably over time, much of it taking place outside municipal boundaries. However, several aspects of the expansion have often been unplanned. One reason is the lack of an integrated development plan of the city and a regional/subregional plan that is based on a long-term economic vision that outlines key long-term goals, identifies sectors and activities that are expected to drive the local economy, and specifies the public inputs that must be provided for enterprises to thrive. The stakeholder consultations showed that an economic vision with these elements has not been drawn up in the 12 study cites.

Without an economic vision in place to guide decision making, urban areas have grown without leaving sufficient space for right-of-ways and provision of basic infrastructure. Without adequate planning and "visioning," the city infrastructure becomes stressed, leading to congestion, uneven access to basic utility infrastructure and services, susceptibility to weather-related events such as flooding, and high land prices for both businesses and households. Issues such as these are adversely affecting the economic dynamism of cities.

Figure 5.1: Key Bottlenecks that Constrain Cities from Realizing their Economic Potential

Key Problem Areas

1. Absence of common economic vision
2. Locational disadvantages
   - Lack of regional linkages because of terrain issues
   - Environmental risks/constraints for flooding, drought, etc.
3. Economic growth hampered by lack of historical industrial base
4. Inadequate financial support for government-led industrial development, due to elevated land prices
5. Issues related to land supply
   - Challenges in acquiring large land parcels for major projects.
   - Challenges with costs and processes associated with converting land from non urban to urban use
6. Procedural challenges such as titling, acquisition and aggregation, land conversion, etc.
7. Lack of economic inputs to the master planning exercise
   - Lack of department-level forward-looking master plans
   - MSMEs' needs not considered while planning for industrial development
8. Absence of integrated planning of industrial infrastructure
   - Connectivity infrastructure is lacking between industrial and residential areas ("last mile connectivity")
   - Absence of good quality utility infrastructure; lack of 24x7 uninterrupted power supply
9. Inadequate provision of affordable and rental housing for workers around key economic centers
10. Multiplicity of agencies involved in similar charter of work
11. Interdepartment coordination issues
    - Coordination mechanism between/with state govt. departments and urban local bodies is not synchronized or aligned with center and state strategic priorities
    - Coordination issues between/with departments at the same level
12. Capacity constraints
    - Lack of planning capacity and institutional knowledge and/or limited capacity of organizations
13. Issues related to ease of doing business
    - Current approval processes from pollution control board, etc., deter private-sector-led investment
14. Service-level delivery aspects are absent
15. Framework for engaging and leveraging private sector efficiencies is missing
    - Clear policy framework/standard documents are missing, elevating the perception of risk associated with investment
16. Regulatory constraints
    - Lack of regulations to relocate elsewhere the traditional polluting industries within the city
17. Framework for positioning the state to investors and promoting investments in the state
    - Lack of specialized knowledge on how to position the state to investors

MSMEs = micro, small, and medium-sized enterprises.
Source: Study team.

In fact, the absence of an economic vision at the city level appears to be closely connected to several other bottlenecks identified in the cities. For example, without an economic vision, city master planning exercises tend to focus entirely on land-use and spatial and zoning regulations and do not inform infrastructure investment plans needed to realize economic goals. Similarly, the absence of a well-articulated economic vision for the city implies that economic visioning exercises carried out at the state level by state industry and planning departments may lack an explicit spatial dimension that can serve as an anchor for agencies focusing on urban development.

Challenges Related to Land

As India urbanizes, issues pertaining to the acquisition, use, and development of urban and peri-urban land have emerged as an important and urgent problem for governments at all levels. Land is expensive in most metropolitan urban centers and the acquisition and development of large land parcels for key urban projects is challenging. Even in smaller urban centers where the cost of land might not be the largest constraint, bottlenecks related to processes associated with acquiring and aggregating land for new developments and projects and change of land use are present. Challenges around land use, particularly in the urban context, are complex and multi-layered in the study cities and in other Indian cities.

As India's economy and population continue to grow, serviced urban land is becoming increasingly scarce and competing claims are made on a finite supply. In addition, land acquisition on the urban periphery also triggers an economic transition from an agrarian-based economy to one that is increasingly dominated by secondary or tertiary industries (Sami 2011). If this happens in an unplanned way, such areas tend to develop as an unmanageable sprawl devoid of basic facilities.

Factors that make land availability a challenge include (i) the inadequacy of land records; and (ii) the processes and costs associated with land acquisition, conversion, and aggregation. Such challenges must be solved to avoid unwarranted delays and costs in development projects and private sector ventures that boost the economy and employment.

Land records system. India's land records were created with the specific intent of generating revenue in rural and agricultural areas (Goswami et al. 2021). Consequently, records in urban or densely settled areas are often not detailed. This hampers transfer and conversion of land titles.

In some cases, there may as yet be no title, and land ownership is often by "presumptive title": property ownership arising through occupation or possession of the land rather than possession of an ownership document or other apparent right. Further, the operation of informal and sometimes illegal mechanisms of land transfer renders even the most detailed urban planning efforts ineffective and developmental controls become difficult to enforce (Ramanathan 2009).

To acquire land for developing infrastructure (or an industrial/business park for that matter) requires that land ownership records are clear. Thus, a clear and transparent process of urban land records is needed. However, records of urban and peri-urban land are held by various state and municipal agencies and are difficult to reconcile. In particular, the land survey department prepares spatial/cadastral maps, the land registration department/department of registration and stamps oversees land transactions, the revenue department maintains the Records of Rights, and municipal bodies collect property tax. The presence of multiple authorities complicates and delays the process of land acquisition and conversion. Further, the lack of data sharing between planning, revenue, land survey, and registration departments delays projects in areas transitioning from rural to urban.

Land acquisition. Challenges to acquiring land include costly and complex processes, limited private participation and foreign private equity funding, and competing land uses. In general, the cost and effort of acquiring land for industrial development rests with state governments. After the negative experiences of the 2008 financial crisis, private equity investment has been replaced by mezzanine debt and structured loans via nonbank financial companies that typically do not invest in projects at the land aggregation stage. Competing land uses on the urban periphery, particularly the tension between agricultural and nonagricultural land use, can delay land acquisition.

Conversion. As cities expand outward, some land may need to be reclassified or "converted" (for example from agricultural or residential to industrial uses). However, land conversion is becoming increasingly contentious, particularly in cities such as Guwahati, Indore, Navsari, and Vadodara. The issue of converting land from nonurban to urban uses, especially the tension between agricultural and nonagricultural uses, is a problem on the urban periphery.

Smooth land conversion from agricultural uses also depends on the presence of adequate land records, without which land-use conversion is difficult. Because land records generally do not include details such as land conversion change of use, roadblocks and legal disputes around titles and the nature of the land arise. For several reasons, land conversion cases are time consuming. For example, in Karnataka, such cases are heard only at the High Court level, consequently affecting acquisition timelines.

Aggregation. The aggregation of land to create the contiguous parcels needed for industry may be difficult and time-consuming, given often lengthy negotiations with individual parcel owners and unclear titling. A further complication in the process arises due to unclear boundaries of land parcels. Resolving ambiguities is an extremely important task in the land aggregation process to ensure correct valuation and compensation to owners and needs to be facilitated by integrating geo-referenced cadastral maps in the process.

Lack of Integrated Approach to Master Planning

Introduction

A master plan for an urban area is a statutory document for planning and influencing a city's course of development. This section analyzes the master planning provisions for the industrial development of the cities studied.[61] The analysis enables one to understand the trajectory of planned industrial development, thereby providing the basis for recommendations to sustain and promote economic growth.

---

[61] Given limitations in primary data gathering, most of the findings are based on secondary research. Inputs from stakeholder consultations have been included as relevant.

Key Bottlenecks Constraining the Potential of Cities

A master plan is usually supported by zoning regulations (first instituted in the early decades of the 20th century), which segregate the uses of urban space. The regulations were the principal means for achieving desired urban patterns. Further, a land-use map is an essential component of a master plan. It illustrates the types of development permitted in urban areas and helps with identifying and developing spatial strategies. Master plans usually contain data on the current and proposed land uses and provide land-use maps.

India's current urban planning system owes its origin to the planning institutions and laws established by the British colonial government. The colonial practice of separating urban planning and development from local politics (in the form of city improvement trusts in the pre-independence era) has morphed into the mandate for agencies usually termed "development authorities." Thus, instead of the constitutionally mandated municipal government or the metropolitan planning committee, state-government-controlled development authorities perform the task of urban planning in most of India's major cities (Weinstein et al 2013 and Sami 2012). These institutions, such as the Bangalore Development Authority and the Delhi Development Authority, prepare master plans that regulate land use and development across a city for specific time planning horizons, such as 10–20 years (Idiculla 2021).

As seen in Chapter 3, the spatial footprint of cities has grown considerably over time.[62] Some of this urban expansion has been unplanned, as demonstrated by poor access to urban infrastructure (e.g., sewerage systems and water supply) and industrial infrastructure and weak transport networks. While cities have identified likely expansion areas, the majority of development efforts lack an integrated approach to urban and economic planning in the expansion areas. Only a few cities have tried an integrated approach and incorporated anticipated developments in their planning.

Cities' master plans largely do not articulate development goals based on which actual investments and mixed-use developments can be planned and implemented. The cities are dynamic and expanding rapidly, but the master plans have remained mainly static and account inadequately for future demands for land use and allocations. This has led to inadequate planning of growth-enabling infrastructure.

> *Land parcels earmarked for industrial development do not have adequate relevant trunk infrastructure (including sector-specific industrial infrastructure such as ready-to-use facilities for the electronics sector), resulting in poor uptake by industries.* (Private Industrial Park Developer and Investor)
>
> *Lack of efficient mass transportation services between the industrial areas in the natural city and residential areas in the administrative city have created difficulties for workers.* (Plastic and Plastic Products Manufacturer)

Rigid land-use classifications have compounded the situation. For example, the definition of "industrial development" in city master plans varies widely. Service sector firms, such as those in information technology (IT) and IT-enabled services and start-ups, may not be officially recognized as "industrial" and therefore entitled to land allocation. Because many master plans do not make land-use provisions

---

[62] For example, Warangal natural city grew by 62% from 2000 to 2016 while Vijayawada natural city had grown by 240% by 2016. The natural city areas were substantially larger than their administrative counterparts as captured through the 2011 Census of India data: 229 square kilometers (km^2) versus 141 km^2 for Warangal and 978 km^2 versus 165 km^2 for Indore (ORGCC n.d.).

for them, such firms often work in an isolated manner and do not form an integral part of the city's growth strategy. Rigid land-use classification has also led to increased demand for affordable and organized housing going unmet.

Challenges with City Master Plans

Each of the cities analyzed as part of this study has developed distinctly within its historic and geo-spatial context. The cities have also undertaken master planning exercises to varying degrees under the direction of development authorities. The following paragraphs describe four issues that were common across the cities studied from the perspective of planned industrial development.

Weak links between master plans and economic goals. Most master plans studied focus on population projections and provision of land, mobility, and housing. A few master plans, such as those for Gangtok and Machilipatnam, explicitly mention economic development goals as an essential part of their vision. However, their master plans are not optimally integrated with the cities' economic goals and do not offer the corresponding investment plans needed to realize such goals. Further, the master planning is often limited to land use, road networks, and building rules and focus on controlling growth instead of initiating and encouraging it. This impedes planned growth and skews development.

However, some state governments do actively support industrial development plans being outlined in their master plans through appropriate legislative, bureaucratic, and financial support. Examples are the development of the Kakatiya Mega Textile Park (a Warangal master plan initiative) and the Dewas–Indore–Mhou–Pithampur super region development (outlined in their master plans). These examples show how city governments can proactively work with longer-term strategies on issues of economic importance.

Limitations in land-use classifications. The definition of "industries" in the master plans studied varies widely. In general, manufacturing is adequately represented within the categories permitted for industrial land uses. The definition is both an enabler and a constraint. As an enabler, it allows identified lands to develop industrial assets. However, the definition can be a constraint when sectors or activities such as IT and research and development units and start-ups that are economically influential are not defined as "industrial." Because many master plans do not make land allocation provisions for such enterprises, short-term solutions such as integrated industrial parks and software technology parks are created. But, as a result, such enterprises often work in isolation rather than forming an integral part of the city's growth strategy. The Electronic City Area, a specially defined and governed industrial development area in Bengaluru, is a case in point (Sood 2015).

Further, because the land-use definitions are updated only when master plans are updated (or prepared)—once in about 15–20 years—they become redundant and less than helpful in the wake of scientific and technological advances allied with industrial development. As a result, new types of industries struggle to get the needed approvals and find land allocations and support.

Rigidities in land-use allocation. Analysis of land-use plans and land allocations indicated that the projections of future demand by the town and country planning departments and embedded in master plans are often mismatched with the actual, realized demand. The "project and provide" approach of master plans often does not meet the growth demands of or provide incentives to cities that are fast growing. In addition, land allocation strategies are slow to respond to market forces and

Key Bottlenecks Constraining the Potential of Cities

local aspirations and trends. Modelling future demands and growth is useful, but not always fail-proof. For example, advancements in industrial engineering and technology often challenge projections. While cities are dynamic and open ended, the master plans are static.

Lack of regional strategy and spatial planning mechanisms. As seen clearly in Chapter 3, cities often expand dramatically beyond their administrative boundaries, with their economic drivers partly outside these boundaries. Further, the urban and economic footprint of cities can straddle multiple administrative units. Accordingly, spatial planning needs to be carried out in a regional context. Currently, this approach is missing.

Inadequate Institutional Frameworks and Capacity Constraints

As illustrated in Chapter 3, natural cities often cover multiple administrative units. For example, in 2016, Vadodara's natural city crossed two districts and 19 towns and Vijayawada's natural city encompassed three districts and 14 towns. This clearly calls for cross-jurisdiction governance to effectively manage cities and their periphery, but such governance is absent across the study cities. Further, multiple stakeholders or institutions even within the same jurisdictions may have overlapping functions or responsibilities that conflict with each other, leading to fragmented governance and unclear accountability.

Additionally, there is insufficient coordination between agencies involved in industrial and economic planning, infrastructure planning, and urban planning and management. The result is a significant disconnect between urban governance processes and economic processes, resulting in a mismatch between urban priorities and economic ones. For example, state government departments and their counterparts responsible for transport, housing, and water supply and sanitation often take a sector-specific approach to planning and operations. This has led these agencies to work in sectoral silos with little integrated infrastructure planning or service provision in the city. Further, the existence of multiple actors and overlapping jurisdictions also leads to a lack of coordination and fragmentation of powers and responsibilities, contributing to delays in project development and suboptimal delivery of services.

A crucial issue is that city governments play a limited role in influencing and coordinating the work of different agencies at the local level and even less in guiding economic development. Devolution of power to urban local bodies (ULBs) is mandated by the 74th Constitutional Amendment—which provides guidelines on decentralization and expects states to empower ULBs by devolving adequate powers, finances, and responsibilities to them (Sami 2013). But the devolution has been incomplete and uneven across the country, despite being mandated through the first generation of urban reform programs.[63] Instead, ULBs in India primarily deal with providing basic urban services and depend heavily on the state and central governments to finance infrastructure development and provide key social amenities. They do not have the functions or responsibilities to attract investments, nor a mandate to provide the ancillary and supporting infrastructure for fostering local economic development.

---

[63] Despite the devolution of power to ULBs provided in the 74th Constitutional Amendment Act (1992), the implementation has been piecemeal (Sami 2013). In most Indian states, "the local or city government has little autonomy in decision making (Sami 2013: 125). Most of this power rests with the state government—the devolution of responsibilities and power is at the discretion of the state government. The powers that ULBs have, therefore, are not the same across the country because state governments have not uniformly devolved power. Thus, it is challenging for ULBs to be proactive about reform because they lack the authority to take and implement their decisions.

This has limited the capacity and ability of India's cities to actively direct and manage economic transformation, in sharp contrast with cities in a wide range of middle- and high-income countries, which tend to have much more say in functions related to economic development. For example, in the United States, local governments use a range of tools to attract investment and nurture business, including marketing and promotion activities; tax and other financial incentives; land-related incentives, for example, through land rezoning and land acquisition; infrastructure upgrades; and regulations, for example, through improved processes for building inspections (Wolman and Spitzley 1996). Similarly, in the People's Republic of China, local governments have strong incentives and authority to formulate and implement plans for economic development and attracting private investment. Further, tax-sharing reforms implemented in 1994 have given local governments a share in the collection of value-added tax (among others); thus, local governments seek to attract investment to bolster their tax base by improving local infrastructure, providing land, and even negotiating with the central government to exempt businesses from regulations (ADB 2019).

Finally, ULBs have few personnel trained and adequate to keep pace with urban growth, leading to ULBs' inability to meet current needs and plan for future growth. Despite the fact that Indian cities face complex challenges that cut across sectors and domains (economic and environmental, for example), many urban functionaries do not have enough technical background, support, tools, processes, or access to training programs that could enable them to respond to new challenges. ULBs do not have sufficient capacity to work with multiple stakeholders (including public and private stakeholders across national, regional, and local levels) as well as to interact regularly with local communities in their jurisdiction.

Business-Related Policies and Regulatory Constraints

The policy and regulatory framework that firms face at any given location in India is influenced primarily by the central and relevant state governments.[64] For example, tariff rates are set by the central government in accordance with its trade policy, labor laws are set by both the central and state governments, and the development of industrial and business parks—a feature of industrial policy—tends to be taken at the state level. Similarly, various types of incentives and programs are provided by central and state governments to attract investments into a sector and or region. Table 5.1 describes key ones for manufacturing.[65]

---

[64] Policies and regulations are important tools governments have to influence economic development in their jurisdictions. While policies provide focus and direction to help a government achieve its goals, regulations are administrative in nature and are designed to make enterprises and individuals comply in a manner desired by government.

[65] A prominent example at the central level is the recent production-linked incentive scheme that provides firms with financial incentives for making large-scale investments in selected manufacturing subsectors. States also promote investments. In Karnataka, for example, the state government introduced an investment scheme for designing and manufacturing electronics systems—the scheme provides subsidies for procuring land in locations beyond the Bengaluru region and for investing in plant and machinery.

Table 5.1: Incentives in India for Manufacturing

Type	Land, Infrastructure, and Amenities Subsidy	Tax Exemptions/ Rebates	Targeted Incentives	Credit-Linked Subsidies
Specific Incentives Provided in Policies	Capital investment subsidy, plant and machinery expansion and upgrade subsidy, electricity and water tariff exemption/rebate, concessional land rates, common infrastructure/cluster development schemes	Tax and stamp duty exemptions and rebates, SGST and CGST rebates, electricity duty rebate, Mandi tax exemption, export/import tax exemptions	Production/turn-over-linked subsidies, incentives for incremental sales, results-based financing subsidies	Interest payment subsidies, subsidies on loans for MSMEs and other target sectors, loan guarantees
Relevance	• Increase a region's attractiveness for setting up businesses • Make a sector/region accessible to new firms through capital subsidies	Lower the cost of operating business and increase the return on investments, making the region more attractive	Increase the contribution of a sector/type of firm by incentivizing them to produce more	Reduce the entry barriers for high-capital-expenditure businesses by increasing the access to finance

CGST = central government sales tax; MSMEs = micro, small, and medium-sized enterprises; SGST = state general sales tax.
Note: Mandi tax is a fee levied to support running agricultural wholesale markets.
Source: Study Team.

ULBs have played a limited role in contributing to the design of these incentives and programs and to their effectiveness—for example, by taking early action to complement them. As noted in the previous section, this is because responsibility for local economic development does not rest with ULBs in practice. Thus, it is not surprising that the cities studied lack a dedicated strategy to promote themselves proactively and attract investments, with the possible exception of Indore, which promotes itself as the cleanest city in India.

However, one way city-level governments or ULBs do influence the business environment is by setting development norms to which businesses must adhere, thereby influencing the ease of starting and operating businesses. Discussions with private sector stakeholders indicated that a majority of them faced challenges in doing business in the study cities. Further, the discussions revealed that cities could improve the "ease of doing business"—just as the center and states have been doing.[66]

> *While there is a single window clearance mechanism, several services and approvals related to [ease of doing business], such as electricity connection, pollution board approval, and fire-safety-related no-objection clearances, require approvals from different authorities and are time-consuming to obtain* (Large Food Processing Conglomerate).

While a single window system at the state level has brought most of the approvals required to set up a manufacturing facility under one platform, for the services industry and for setting up local businesses such as hotels, restaurants, and hospitals at the ULB level, the number of approvals the entrepreneur needs and the time invested are considerably more than in global counterparts. Setting up a hotel at the city level is a case in point (Box 5.1).

---

[66] India has made rapid progress on the regulatory front. Rules and regulations especially on foreign investments have been simplified. Further, technology has been used to simplify regulatory processes for aspects of doing business such as company registration, customs, and taxation. In particular, the regulatory environment has been simplified for (i) starting a business, (ii) trading across borders (customs processes), (iii) resolving insolvency (primarily on account of progressive laws such as insolvency and bankruptcy laws), and (iv) dealing with construction permits (Government of India 2020).

> ### Box 5.1: Setting Up a Hotel in a City
>
> **Ease and cost of doing business.** From a regulatory and operational point of view, to set up a hotel in India the investor must
> - acquire land, which involves land conversion unless the land is already registered for commercial purposes;
> - secure preoperation licenses and approvals; and
> - meet tax and operational compliance requirements.
>
> **Land acquisition.** Land is an important part of a hotel's capital investment. As acquiring land inside a city is increasingly difficult due to availability and cost, some hotels are moving outside cities while in some cases hotels are being allowed in residential areas.
>
> **Preoperations licenses and approvals.** After acquiring the land, numerous approvals and licenses are needed to set up a hotel or restaurant. Moreover, in India only a few licenses and permissions can be applied for online, thus requiring an entrepreneur to visit various offices physically to obtain the licenses and permissions. For example, 23 approvals are required at the state level to open a hotel in Maharashtra; in Karnataka the number is 21, in Tamil Nadu it is 19, and in Gujarat it is 16.[a]
>
> Also, the approvals need to be received from multiple departments at local, state, and central levels and using different portals, making the process cumbersome. Additional specific issues may also add to costs. For example, in Mumbai no distinction is made between an entertainment event, such as a fashion show or concert, and a corporate event, such as an award function. The larger number of permissions needed for an entertainment event applies to business conferences as well, raising costs for the latter.
>
> [a] These approvals are based on the National Single Window System, a digital platform for guiding investors on approvals pertaining to their sector of interest (https://www.nsws.gov.in/). The Study Team used the platform to understand the approvals needed to set up a hotel in the study states in October 2022, including approvals required for providing lift services, operating standard kitchens, and serving liquor.
> Source: Study Team.

In summary, high land acquisition costs, the many approvals from multiple departments, time-consuming procedures, and nonuniform tax structures are inhibiting setting up hotels in India as well as other local services such as hospitals and malls. Addressing these issues is important to enhance the ease of doing business in Indian cities.

More generally, a framework for engaging with the private sector is missing across cities.[67] This is problematic as officials, businesses, and residents of cities are likely to have detailed knowledge and understanding about their locations as places to do business. City planners and governments need to acquire this understanding in order to attract economic activity, especially given the mobility of capital across cities (Peterson 1981 cited and quoted in Wolman and Spitzley 1996).

---

[67] Some cities need an approach to deal with historical but polluting manufacturing industries—for example, by moving them from core areas of the city where modern services would be better located. In a few cases, polluting and environmentally hazardous industries have become part of the cities owing to growth in the areas of the cities. Such industries need to be relocated and regulations for enabling relocation need to be set up. The land recovered in this manner needs provisions for redevelopment by the city authorities.

References

Asian Development Bank (ADB). 2019. *Asian Development Outlook 2019 Update: Fostering Growth and Inclusion in Asia's Cities.*

Goswami, A., D. Jha, K. Lushington, M. Yadav, S. Sasidharan, S. Mitra, and T. Wangchuk. 2021. *Land Records Modernisation in India – I.* Indian Institute for Human Settlements. https://doi.org/10.24943/9788195489398 (accessed in December 2021).

Government of India, Ministry of Finance. 2020. Targeting Ease of Doing Business. In Economic Survey 2019–2020 Vol 1. https://www.indiabudget.gov.in/budget2020-21/economicsurvey/doc/vol1chapter/echap06_vol1.pdf.

Idiculla, M. 2021. Who Plans Indian Cities? Development Authorities Who Still Follow Colonial Masterplans. *ThePrint.* https://theprint.in/opinion/who-plans-indian-cities-development-authorities-who-still-follow-colonial-masterplans/770913/ (accessed 24 November 2021).

Office of the Registrar General and Census Commissioner, India (ORGCC). n.d. 2011 Census of India. https://censusindia.gov.in/census.website/ (accessed January–March 2022).

Peterson, P. 1981. *City Limits.* University of Chicago Press.

Ramanathan, S. 2009. Security of Title to Land in Urban Areas. *India Infrastructure Report 2009*, 20.

Sami, N. 2013. From Farming to Development: Urban Coalitions in Pune, India. *International Journal of Urban and Regional Research.* 37(1):151–64.

———. 2012. *Building Alliances: Power and Politics in Urban India.* Doctor of Philosophy, University of Michigan.

———. 2011. *The Political Economy of Urban Land in India: Key Issues.* https://iihs.co.in/knowledge-gateway/wp-content/uploads/2017/05/Political-Economy.pdf.

Sood, A. 2015. Industrial Townships and the Policy Facilitation of Corporate Urbanisation in India. *Urban Studies.* 52(8): 1359–78. https://doi.org/10.1177/0042098014562318 (accessed 13 January 2015).

Weinstein, L., Sami, N. and Shatkin, G. 2013. Contested Developments: Enduring Legacies and Emergent Political Actors in Contemporary Urban India. *In:* Shatkin, G. (ed.) *Contesting the Indian city: Global visions and the politics of the local.* Wiley Blackwell.

Wolman, H., and D. Spitzley. 1996. The Politics of Local Economic Development. *Economic Development Quarterly.* 10(1996):115–50.

Chapter 6

Recommendations

An integrated approach to urban and economic planning is required to address the five areas of bottlenecks to cities' economic growth: lack of an economic vision at the city level; constraints imposed by the supply of land available for development; limitations in master planning; weaknesses in institutional framework and capacity issues, and constraints imposed on business development by policies and regulations. Table 6.1 lists the broad action needed to remove the bottlenecks.

Table 6.1: Action Areas for Removing Bottlenecks to City Economic Growth

Bottleneck	Action Needed
Economic Vision	Develop an integrated economic vision for the city and an institutional structure for implementing the vision
Land Supply	Leverage technology for solving land supply issues and explore alternate land development models
Master Planning	Align demand-driven integrated master planning with economic goals
Institutional Framework and Capacity	Foster institutional integration and build capacity in development and planning
Policies and Regulations	Ensure that the policy and regulatory framework enables and incentivizes local economic development

Source: Authors.

An Economic Vision for the City

An economic vision for cities that outlines the long-term economic goals and identifies promising sectors and activities for driving the local economy can play a crucial role in guiding and coordinating the work of key public city and state agencies. Together such agencies supply various publicly provided inputs that enterprises need to thrive (Box 6.1).

> **Box 6.1: Local Economic Development Strategy for Cities**
>
> Cities such as London, New York, Paris, Singapore, and Tokyo, which are among the top 10 leading destinations for sending and receiving foreign direct investment, do not leave their economic development to chance (Leff and Petersen 2015). They plan for economic development at the city level by formulating local economic development (LED) strategies and they institutionalize this process by setting up and staffing an LED office (NYC 2022).
>
> The LED process builds relationships between local governments, civic organizations, academia, and the private sector to manage resources (human and natural), create jobs, and stimulate a defined area's economy. LEDs function at the intersection of competitiveness, inclusion, and sustainable growth, addressing the various drivers of economic growth. This includes knowledge spillovers, investment complementarity, enabling institutions, effective policy, and even migration management, by training and reemploying the workforce to meet industry demands and provide employment for all. The International Labour Organization and UN HABITAT developed frameworks and manuals for LED as long ago as 2005 (ILO 2014 and UN HABITAT 2005), but they have not been mainstreamed as a process in Indian cities.
>
> Sources: Leff, S., and B. Petersen. 2015. *Beyond the Scorecard: Understanding Global City Rankings*. The Chicago Council on Global Affairs. https://globalaffairs.org/research/report/beyond-scorecardunderstanding-global-city-rankings; Mathews, R., A. Kundu, P. Chawla, R. Palanichamy, M. Pai, and T. Sebastian. Forthcoming. *Evolution and Morphology of Delhi- National Capital Region's Economic Geography and Implications for Planning*. World Resources Institute; New York City (NYC). 2022. *Rebuild, Renew, Reinvent: A Blueprint for New York City's Economic Recovery*. New York City Economic Development Corporation (NYC EDC) n.d. NYC Difference. Economic Development Corporation. https://edc.nyc/why-nyc#:~:text=With%20a%20gross%20metropolitan%20product,countries%20like%20Canada%20and%20Russia.

The starting point for developing a city's economic vision is the economic vision of its state. The latter describes the state's developmental aspirations and macro targets for economic growth and identifies sectors and activities that currently drive the economy and are expected to do so for the next 10–15 years. The broad contours of a city-specific economic vision can be drawn by mapping state-level policy and sectoral priorities to specific locations in the state—i.e., the urban (or rural) centers where firms belonging to specific manufacturing and services subsectors are located, or where new investments are expected to locate.

For example, a recent report of the Madhya Pradesh State Policy and Planning Commission identifies sectors and activities that have done well and/or hold promise (Government of Madhya Pradesh 2022). Examples are food processing, labor-intensive manufacturing, pharmaceuticals and biomedical devices, and information-technology-enabled services; and examples of activities include research and development and incubation hubs for start-ups, skills development, and exports for instilling dynamism. Significantly, the report calls for a "growth center" approach that focuses on key urban agglomerations in the state (including the Indore and Dewas region). The report also calls attention to specific infrastructure and policy needs, such as developing logistics infrastructure; improving urban planning; providing an "ecosystem" that can support micro, small, and medium-sized enterprises in their business development needs; and attracting foreign direct investment.

Beyond this, developing a city-level economic vision requires further steps, including thinking about the institutional framework that would underlie the development and implementation of the vision. Box 6.2 summarizes how six international cities developed and implemented plans for their economic development and the institutional frameworks that played a key role in their journeys.

Box 6.2: Six Cities' Growth Visions, Actions, and Outcomes

Case studies of six cities (Cape Town, South Africa; London, United Kingdom; Malmö, Sweden; Seoul, Republic of Korea; Singapore; and Zurich, Switzerland) are described below.

Cape Town, South Africa

Insights on the plan developed. Cape Town has created a comprehensive vision, "OneCape2040," for the city to become "one of the world's greatest cities in which to live and learn, work, invest and discover." As part of its Vision 2040, the "Central City Development Strategy," a 10-year vision for the future sustainable and inclusive development, was developed and launched in 2012–2013.

Institutional setup to promote economic development. The initiatives to achieve the OneCape2040 vison are implemented by Cape Town's Transport and Urban Development Authority. The Authority has been enabled to undertake all urban and economic development activities in the province of Cape Town, including developing and executing the urban and economic development plans.

Initiatives to enable private and local stakeholders' participation. As part of the vision, Cape Town developed a social development strategy and created the Public Participation Unit in collaboration with various directorates to help build an inclusive and vibrant city. For the infrastructure development plans, public needs analysis is done through community satisfaction surveys.

Impact. The impact is seen in terms of private sector employers setting up shop or expanding in the city and a decline in Cape Town's unemployment rate—which dropped from 24.9% in 2012 to 22.1% in 2015.

London, United Kingdom

Insights on the plan developed. The City of London was able to keep its place as a global hub for financial and business services because of the vision of economic development created by its mayors. The vision introduces new ideas while maintaining continuity from the previous action plans and vision. The initiatives of the current vision (created in 2017 by the then mayor) range from inclusive development to better urban services to cost of living and attracting talent.

Institutional setup to promote economic development. London's economic development is led by the mayor. All the key functions, including infrastructure and transport, are with the mayor's office. This has minimized coordination efforts and decision-making time.

Initiatives to enable private and local stakeholders' participation. The city council, led by the mayor, has specific programs to include and consults subject matter experts. This leads to a current view of requirements incorporating the ideas of the pertinent industry, subject matter experts, and civic society in development initiatives and governance issues.

Impact. London successfully kept and strengthened its place in the world as a hub for financial and business services.

Malmö, Sweden

Insights on the plan developed. Malmö undertook a transformational journey from a city dependent on the shipbuilding industry to a center for sustainable development, industries, and research. This happened because a carefully curated plan was created and implemented by the city council in the 1990s and 2000s with participation from civic society and industries.

Institutional setup to promote economic development. The principle of local self-government is guaranteed in the Swedish constitution. The local council is led by the city mayor, who is responsible for

continued on next page

Box 6.2 *continued*

developing and executing the city's economic vision. The council has been credited with turning the city around from being a declining shipbuilding city to being a modern center for sustainable development and growth. An important element in the successful change was devolving power to district leadership within the city.

Initiatives to enable private and local stakeholders' participation. As part of the turnaround, the well-being of residents was prioritized. To encourage young creators to move to Malmö, a new university was started. The city has converted polluted areas into sustainable housing projects and provided laboratories for testing clean technologies. Many promotional and awareness activities were launched to attract the talent and visitors.

Impact. The city of Malmö is now known in Sweden and Europe as a center for sustainable development. This resulted from the careful creation and implementation of a forward-looking economic development vision, planning for decades in the future.

Seoul, Republic of Korea

Insights into the plan developed. Economic and urban planning was done in three key phases, the 1960s and 1970s; 1980s and 1990s; and 2000s and beyond, focusing on 10-year targets and using real estate as a growth lever for planning urban and economic growth of the city. Further, in 2015 a 100-year urban planning framework was initiated.

Institutional setup to promote economic development. The Seoul Metropolitan Government (SMG) is responsible for urban and economic planning. The SMG includes administrative leadership, political leadership, and the participation of civil society. This stakeholder setup has enabled and empowered the SMG because it has

- information about the aspirations and requirements of civic society for the development of the city,
- the economic and financial resources to carry out development work,
- civic society buy-in for the development and growth trajectory, and
- political buy-in for development initiatives.

Initiatives to enable private and local stakeholders' participation. The SMG has dedicated initiatives and arrangements for civic society participation. The SMG has developed into a successful metropolitan government that works effectively to recognize local concerns and policy decision-making processes of lower-level governments and then incorporate them into the governance process.

Impact. Although Seoul was in ruins during the 1950s, it was turned into a global metropolis within half a century with the support of rapid economic growth. During this period, Seoul overcame various urban problems to grow and advance into a "smart city" where 10 million people live comfortably.

Singapore

Insights on the plan developed. Singapore's development strategy is to build on its strengths and let go of unsuitable growth opportunities. Planning and a phased, integrated approach with regular monitoring is a key.

Singapore's Economic Development Board (EDB) undertook 10-year plans for the country's economic growth. (i) In the 1960s and 1970s, Singapore focused on establishing the manufacturing sector. (ii) In the 1908s, the focus was on establishing the information technology sector by providing favorable investment incentives, policies, and facilitation for information technology companies and skill development via the country's National Computer Board. (iii) In the 1990s, the focus was on ensuring that Singapore became a center for high-tech services with the help of the National University of Singapore, the Nanyang Technical University, and other science-based institutes.

continued on next page

Box 6.2 *continued*

Institutional setup to promote economic development. The State and City Planning Project was launched and completed in 1971 to address the need for adequate housing and the generation of employment opportunities for citizens. Singapore's first concept plan was prepared to guide the city–state's physical development for the next 20 years. This task was subsequently undertaken by the Urban Redevelopment Authority (URA).

The URA works with the EDB to ensure that the country's urban development is aligned with its economic development. The EDB is designed as a focal agency for attracting and facilitating investment and laying down the long-term economic development roadmap for the country.

Initiatives to enable private and local stakeholders' participation. Private sector participation is built into the EDB's structure. It comprises executive management; board members with a chairman; a consulting company; a strategist; representation for education, business, and corporate society; an international advisory council; and chief executives of top companies

Impact. Singapore created an agile, feasible, and aspirational economic vision with defined targets by building on existing strengths, growing new capabilities, and shifting away from activities that were no longer viable. This was supported directly by Prime Minister Lee Kuan Yew, who empowered agencies such as the EDB and URA to independently formulate and implement the development visions.

A dedicated agency is the key for the development and implementation of an economic vision aligned with urban development. In Singapore's case, the URA has been instrumental in bringing about the impressive change in the city–state's physical landscape since independence, with periodic and forward-looking planning.

Zurich, Switzerland

Insights on the plan developed. The city council under the mayor's office created a vision 2035 in 2007. In 2011 the City Council revised the vision's strategies and brought them up to date. In 2014 an appraisal looked at whether the goals had been reached and how relevant they still were for the development of the city. The "Zurich Strategies 2035" provides the City Council with long-term direction and orientation for its activities and helps the council determine which work areas to focus on.

Institutional setup to promote economic development. The mayor's office's responsibilities and departments include civic services (births, deaths, and marriages as well as residents' registration), and has offices for the archives; statistics; cultural affairs; and urban development, which includes city and neighborhood development, cross-cultural issues, economic development, and foreign affairs.

The mayor's department is also responsible for promoting economic and political interests in the city, both at home and abroad. The mayor's office provides services for industry clusters, start-ups and entrepreneurships, and economic development.

Initiatives to enable private and local stakeholders' participation. As part of the revision of Zurich's strategies, the city council continues to interact and engage with the private sector in several key areas: infrastructure development for new upcoming industrial sectors, services to promote start-ups, and entrepreneurship; urban services; and urban infrastructure. This private sector participation has led to revision of the 2035 strategies, keeping them current and relevant.

Impact. Zurich is consistently recognized as one of the most livable cities in the world, primarily because of its excellent urban services, urban infrastructure, and employment opportunities for highly skilled talent in financial and business services.

Source: Study Team.

The international experience and stakeholder consultations carried out for this study indicate that the following steps and issues should be considered for developing a comprehensive economic vision for a city over a long-term horizon (10–15 years). Critically, the vision must extend well beyond the administrative boundaries of the city to a broader concept, such as the "natural city," and encompass multiple local government units.

(i) Establish geographic, demographic, and thematic priorities by identifying (a) industries and sectors where the city can be competitive, and (b) geographic areas that will drive the investments and growth of these sectors. A good guiding question for this exercise is to ask: *What could the city be famous for?*

(ii) Outline the key enablers needed—such as infrastructure, skills, appropriately located land, access to business development services, and streamlined compliance processes. A good guiding question for this exercise is to ask: *Why is the city not famous for this industry/sector already?*[68]

(iii) Assess the resources and efforts required to provide the key enablers.

(iv) Define the roles and responsibilities of stakeholders—industry bodies, start-ups, investors, developers, and government.

(v) Ensure that the economic vision exercise and master planning are consistent with one another and compatible in terms of time and planning horizon. (The city master plan itself should be developed through intensive consultations with multiple stakeholders from many sectors.)

(vi) Devise an action plan for developing and disseminating the economic vision, obtaining feedback, and implementing the plan.

To carry out the foregoing steps, an institutional mechanism is needed. Based on international experience, a city economic council (CEC) can play this role.[69] Further, CECs can play a key role in implementing the strategy of local economic development proposed by many experts.

Supported by representatives from leading industries, academics, economic experts, and worker associations, the CEC would:

---

[68] A systematic approach is needed to answer both questions. Specifically, it is important to be realistic about what the city can be famous for and what exactly prevents the city for becoming famous without support from public agencies. Typically, cities can become famous in sectors wherein they have some latent comparative advantage and by correcting market failure(s) that prevent the cities from thriving in the first place. For example, a city may have historical/cultural sites that could form the locus for a vibrant tourism industry, but poor connectivity prevents the industry from emerging. Similarly, firms belonging to a particular manufacturing subsector may exist in the city, but they may face difficulties in expanding further (for example, due to lack of land) and/or diversifying into similar products with greater demand, regionally or even globally (for example, due to lack of specialized skills and infrastructure). For a comprehensive discussion of how governments should approach the goal of developing certain regions/locations, see Grover, Lall, and Maloney (2022).

[69] CECs were also proposed in NITI Aayog (2018), which noted that each city should be recognized as a distinct unit of the economy with the councils serving as a bridge between business and local and state governments to catalyze investments into the city. Particularly in larger cities, CECs would serve as a bridge between businesses and city/state governments to improve the ease of doing business and catalyze investments in the city.

(i) contribute to the development of the economic vision and strategy for promoting local economic development,

(ii) coordinate with the relevant stakeholders to ensure integrated development meets the objectives of the vision,

(iii) define key performance indicators and monitor the outcomes of the economic vision on a regular basis, and

(iv) promote and drive investments around the focus sectors.

The governance structure of the CEC needs to be worked out on a case-by-case basis, taking into account city characteristics (for example, is it a capital city of a state, a large natural city, or a small city) and the administrative structures and frameworks in place in the state. Figure 6.1 presents one possible model for governance of a CEC for a smaller city, with the following broad features.[70]

(i) The CEC is housed at the level of the urban local body (ULB) or district administration. Accordingly, it would be chaired by the city municipal commissioner, district collector, and/or the head of the urban development authority, with all of these officials also taking an active role in disseminating the economic vision across stakeholders.

(ii) A representative of local industry should cochair the CEC along with the government representative to make it a private-sector- and investor-driven initiative.

(iii) The minister of industry and urban departments should review the implementation of the economic vision annually.

The development of a CEC needs to go hand-in-hand with broader capacity-building programs for key stakeholders. Thus, while a program is needed for developing the capacity to plan, manage, and implement an economic vision, including for district collectors and development authority officers, building the capacity of officials in urban development and planning departments is equally important (NITI Aayog 2021).[71]

---

[70] In the case of a capital city, the chair should likely be a very senior official. For example, in the Mumbai Metropolitan Regional Development Authority, the Chief Minister is the chairperson.

[71] NITI Aayog (2021) recommended the following actions for capacity building by the state governments to enhance their ability for urban development: (i) hire an adequate number of permanent or contractual staff in ULBs and development authorities and town and country planning departments; (ii) ensure that qualified professionals—urban planners, urban designers, urban economists, etc.—are hired for urban planning tasks; (iii) mainstream capacity-building activities by assigning an annual budget and linking the training with the career progress of officers and staff; and (iv) for long-term transformation, constitute a "high-powered committee" to reengineer the urban-planning governance structure to (a) define a clear division of roles and responsibilities among various authorities, handle appropriate revision of rules and regulations, etc.; (b) create a more dynamic organizational structure and standardize job descriptions of town planners and other experts; and (c) enable extensive adoption of technology for enabling public participation and interagency coordination.

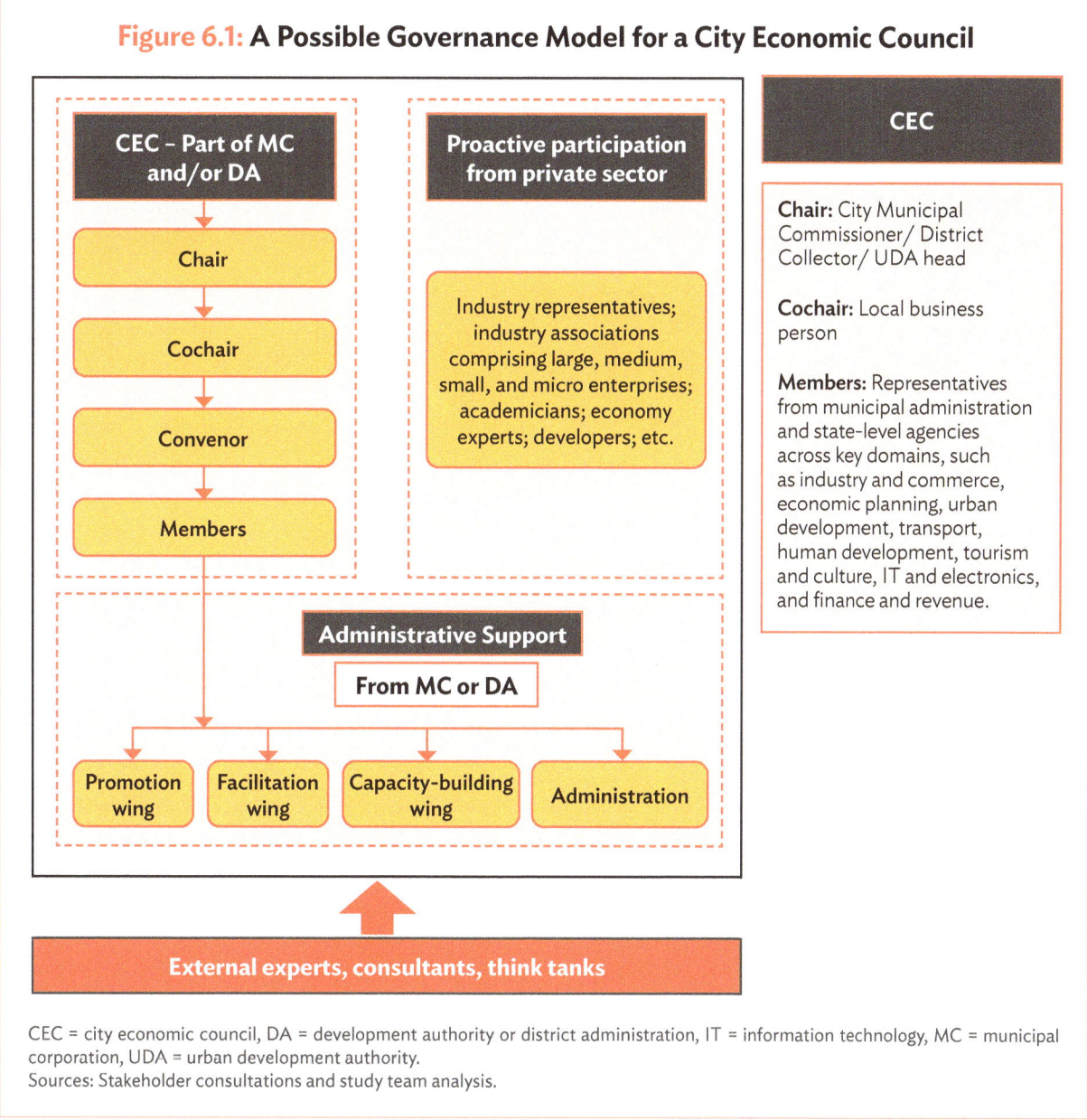

Figure 6.1: A Possible Governance Model for a City Economic Council

CEC = city economic council, DA = development authority or district administration, IT = information technology, MC = municipal corporation, UDA = urban development authority.
Sources: Stakeholder consultations and study team analysis.

Land Supply for Enabling Development

To address the challenges that land-related issues pose to economic development in urban and peri-urban areas, two promising approaches are to improve land records systems and for state governments to develop "investor-ready" land banks.

Initiatives to Improve Land Records Systems

To address inefficiencies in the functioning of land markets, land records systems need to be improved. Revenue, registration, ULBs, and survey functions at the state level need to be integrated institutionally to harmonize land records data. This is needed to (i) enable data sharing across departments, (ii) decrease discrepancies in the transaction processes, and (iii) reduce instances of litigation.

Technology platforms must be integrated to improve the efficiency of land transactions. Portals are needed for showcasing the inventory of land parcels and enabling global information system (GIS) tagging for online viewing and procurement. The use of digital technologies is critical to creating workable and integrated technology platforms that include the flexibility to deal with different types of data and a range of complex "on-the-ground" processes.

The Government of India considers land record management an important area of intervention. The Union Budget 2023[72] stresses the importance of the efficient use of land resources. The Budget encourages states to adopt a unique land parcel identification number to facilitate IT-based records management and roll out a facility for transliteration of land records across all of India's official languages. To implement this initiative, "One-Nation One-Registration Software" is to be introduced for a uniform process of registering deeds and documents, including those pertaining to land.

A variety of initiatives are also being undertaken across states to improve systems of land records.

- **Tamil Nadu** has created unique identifications (IDs) for land parcels. The ID system will identify land parcels with a unique land parcel ID number rather than survey numbers. This is a step toward better management of land using IT. It will allow for integrated data sharing across departments and will deliver services through a single window system. Because the system is still in the process of implementation, little information regarding it is available in the public domain.

- In **Haryana**, the computerization of land records through a twinned bridged system has allowed smooth service delivery. In addition, technological linking of the Haryana Registration Information System and the Haryana Land Records Information System has allowed changes of land records to be updated within 30 days.

- **Karnataka** undertook a large-scale computerization of land records. As part of this, manual records were made invalid in the year 2000, ensuring that all changes in land records are digitized through the Bhoomi initiative. Banks and land acquisition authorities can access the Bhoomi repository to facilitate verification and planning processes. The Bhoomi is linked to the registration software, Karnataka Valuation and e-Registration, ensuring cross-verification processes.

- **Maharashtra** has digitized legacy records of registration and has made the records searchable by property details and available for online download for a fee. This helps prospective buyers trace property transaction history and title records, especially in urban areas where revenue records may not be up to date.

- **Uttar Pradesh's** unique property numbering system helps ease identification of the same property across multiple databases.

---

[72] Government of India. https://www.indiabudget.gov.in/.

Initiatives for Land Aggregation

State government initiatives are needed to develop investor-ready land banks. State governments need to explore financial alternatives to develop good quality land banks. Land banks should be evaluated from several perspectives, including their likely economic, social, and environmental impacts. Participation by private investors or public–private partnership vehicles in the post-acquisition stage should be encouraged.

Land banks could be developed within city limits with the support of the private sector and with specific economic themes, such as information technology parks; fintech hubs; micro, small, and medium-sized enterprise clusters; healthcare; plug-and-play industrial parks; etc. Alternative models for land acquisition and assembly need to be explored. Public participation tools need to be extensively employed, particularly in "Schedule VI States" (those with a preponderance of tribal peoples) so that spatial planning and development is more cohesive. Mechanisms are needed for the speedy redressal of land-related disputes.

Initiatives for large-scale land aggregation and its status have important lessons for similar ventures that are being implemented or planned. Four mechanisms of land aggregation are discussed in the following text.

Ahmedabad, Gujarat: Town Planning Scheme

Ahmadabad follows a town planning scheme (TPS) for aggregating land (IDFC 2010).

Vision. Its vision is to develop Gujarat's largest city, Ahmedabad, using the TPS and to continue to implement it for developing peri-urban areas.

Process. A TPS is a hybrid form of land readjustment where agriculture landowners on the urban fringe give up part of their land in exchange for compensation. Under the TPS, a maximum of 50% of a landowner's agricultural plot is transferred to the government (Sanyal and Deuskar 2012). The government in turn develops civic amenities, raises revenue for infrastructure, and returns reconstituted serviced plots to the original landowners. The state government approves the TPS and local institutions such as the Ahmedabad Municipal Corporation or the Ahmedabad Urban Development Authority propose, draft, and carry out the processes of finalizing the TPS (Deuskar 2011).

Impact. The general advantages of the TPS are that both landowners and government benefit from the process, which is generally seen as a win–win proposition for all parties involved (Sanyal and Deuskar 2012).

Key learning. The TPS is an innovative way of financing public infrastructure. Other cities may need appropriate amendments in their legislative frameworks and to build capacities to adopt this model.

Magarpatta, Maharashtra: Integrated Township

Magarpatta is one of the first new integrated townships built in Maharashtra using the township development model (Deshmukh 2008 and Ganguli 2008).

Vision. The 1982 draft Development Plan for Pune identified the Magarpatta area of the city as a potential location for increasing urban development (Dalal 2008). The farmers, who collectively owned more than 162 hectares (ha)—400 acres—in the region, decided to pool their land and develop it themselves instead of selling it to other developers.

Process. The Magarpatta Township Development and Construction Company (MTDCC) was formed as a private limited company to oversee development and management of the project (Sami 2012). Before forming the company, a variety of models were considered, including a cooperative approach. Using the model adopted, each family received shares proportional to its landholding and was made an equity shareholder. Each share is equal to one square meter of land. The shares of the company may be held and traded among member families only and not publicly traded.

Impact. The planning and design process was essentially managed and controlled by the board of directors. The time needed to get the necessary clearances from the government was used for capacity building. The company promoted and encouraged entrepreneurship among the farmers by providing special training to develop skill sets relating to construction, development, and associated services.

Post-development, most of the families remained on the site and owned apartments or villas that they had bought with the money they made through the company. As shareholders in the MTDCC, they continue to earn a portion of the company's profits. Some of them have rented some of their property, creating another source of income. The land continues to be registered in their names, maintaining ownership and giving them a sense of security. Farming families have managed to move into other occupations.

Key learning. Magarpatta City owes its success largely to three key factors: the favorable economic climate in Pune at the time, the entrepreneurial nature of the Magar community, and the coalitions that one of the farmers—Satish Magar—was able to mobilize by leveraging his social networks (Sami 2012).[73]

Gujarat: Special Investment Region Model

In 2009, Gujarat enacted its Special Investment Region (SIR) Act to enable development of integrated industrial and urban living zones.

Vision. The Gujarat State Government enacted the legal framework to establish, operate, regulate, and manage large investment regions and industrial areas in Gujarat and to enable their development as "global hubs of economic activity supported by world-class infrastructure, premium civic amenities, center of excellence and proactive policy framework."[74]

---

[73] The Magar are a large ethnic group originating from the lower Himalayas and with settlements in many Indian states.
[74] Government of Gujarat (2009:1).

Functional areas. The SIR Act enables the state government to establish, develop, operate, and regulate the SIRs. The government is empowered to declare investment regions or industrial areas and designate them as SIRs. An investment region will have an area of more than 100 square kilometers (km^2) and an industrial area will have an area of more than 50 km^2. An apex authority (the Gujarat Infrastructure Development Board) is provided for by the Act and is the first point of contact for setting up any economic activity or amenity in the SIR. The Board also has final authority on land use and land development plans. A regional development authority is also established under the SIR Act, looks after the "ground-level" issues of development, and can formulate its own regulations for building, construction, and development.

Impact. Gujarat has been able to set up eight SIRs, including the Dholera SIR. Due to the streamlined procedures for developing land conducive for industry, several large-scale businesses have set up in the state, including automobile, chemical, petrochemical, and machinery manufacturing.

Key learning. To remove constraints to development in industrial areas and satellite industrial cities, state governments can develop specific development acts to

- (i) create specific financial packages for the developing industrial areas;
- (ii) customize development norms for each industrial area to meet its needs;
- (iii) create a single window to approve all permissions needed for setting up industries, housing, and other real estate developments; and
- (iv) provide world-class infrastructure relevant for the industries as well as civic amenities.

India: The National Industrial Corridor Development Corporation

The National Industrial Corridor Development Corporation (NICDC) model aims to enable the use of the special purpose vehicle (SPV) model for large-scale development.[75] The NICDC aims to develop industrial nodes in collaboration with state governments.

Vision. The vision is to provide simplified processes for acquiring and developing land for industrial nodes for rapid development and to provide infrastructure for the development of "world-class" industrial townships and cities.

Functional areas. The NICDC relies on the state governments (where industrial nodes have to be developed as part of the planned industrial corridor) for acquiring land parcels for development as industrial townships/modes. This land bank is considered to be the "state's equity in the development SPV" for the node.

The minimum area required for developing an industrial node is 2,000 acres (about 810 ha). The NICDC puts in an amount matching the registration value of the land for infrastructure development purposes. The SPV formed is responsible for creating development norms relevant for the node.

---

[75] For details, see the NICDC website: https://www.nicdc.in/.

Typically, a single window system is also established to support industries with navigating the permissions required for setting up their facilities in the industrial node.

Impact. The time taken to develop the industrial nodes is expected to be reduced by measures such as the single window system.

Key learning. Focus on creating specific bodies for an industrial area, such as a single window system to navigate through the permissions required for setting up industrial units. Develop customized development norms and regulations for industrial areas to suit the requirements of the sectors and industries to be targeted. The development norms need to be flexible to attract investments to the planned industrial areas.

Integrated Master Planning

The following recommendations are provided as a collective strategy for master planning of the cities studied. Individual cities should prioritize the recommendations based on their level of development and specific contexts.

Multisectoral Approach to Spatial Planning

As highlighted by the distinction between administrative and natural cities, the urban fringes and suburban regions of a growing city are key providers of industrial land for development. Further, economic activity in the urban fringes and suburban regions can have an important symbiotic relationship with economic activity within the city—for example, when industry outside the city draws on services located within the city, such as business, housing, and education and health services.

As a result, the larger region, sometimes referred to as a "city–region," needs to be proactively planned, factoring in the needs of both the city and its commuting areas. Among other benefits, integrated planning enables zoning that identifies suitable sites for various categories of industries based on how polluting they are. This can help reduce risks to the environment and procedural delays for investors.

Planning at a city–region level can be useful for enabling the planned expansion of public utilities such as roads and public transport, power lines, and sewerage. City–region-level planning sometimes covers parts of multiple districts, as seen in Chapter 3 with the case of Indore natural city that spanned two districts. The city–region approach is reflected in some recent master plans. For example, the Draft Master Plan 2041 for the Kakatiya Urban Development Area covers 1,805 km^2, which has increased more than 21 times in 5 decades. In Machilipatnam, the area under the Machilipatnam Municipal Corporation is 26.67 km^2, while the area under the Machilipatnam Urban Development Authority is 426.16 km^2.[76]

---

[76] Commissioner and Director of Municipal Administration, Government of Andhra Pradesh. https://cdma.ap.gov.in/node/222#:~:text=Machilipatnam%20municipality%20has%20an%20area,km%20with%2042%20revenue%20wards (accessed 17 July 2022).

More generally, the globe's thriving city–regions demonstrate that the core objective of city–region planning is creating economic opportunities by making growth centers and areas competitive. For example, Ireland attempted this approach for identifying types of regional growth centers with specific expansion targets (such as population growth rates and employment offers) to stimulate industrial development and economic growth (Moseley 1974). Another example of integrative, proactive, and inclusive urban expansion programs is the development of the Tokyo Metropolitan Area in the post-1960s period. The Government of Japan aided the development of the now-famous suburban transit network through measures such as providing subsidies to contractors for constructing network infrastructure and encouraging the holistic development enabled by private railway operators, such as integrated subcenters with social amenities at train stations. As a result, villages and undeveloped lands outside the municipal corporation of Tokyo underwent intensive and supervised transit-oriented development (RIUED 2019).

Allocation of Urban Land to Industrial Uses

Industrial land-use allocation should be tailored to a city's context using an appropriate set of studies, tools, and consultations. The share of area that a city needs as an "industrial" land-use zone may vary widely. Also, some cities may want to limit industrial land use due to concerns about congestion, pollution, or nonconformity of land uses.

The Urban and Regional Development Plans Formulation and Implementation (URDPFI) Guidelines 2015, developed by the Ministry of Urban Development, Government of India, recommends allocating 7%–10% of the developed area of an urban agglomeration to industrial land uses, based on the size and nature of the cities (MOUD 2015). Table 6.2 shows the land-use shares recommended by the URDPFI Guidelines for urban centers.

Table 6.2: Land-Use Structure for Developable Area in Urban Centers

Land-Use Category	Percent of Developed Area			
	Small Cities	Medium Cities	Large Cities	Metropolitan Cities and Megapolises
Residential	45–50	43–48	36–39	36–38
Commercial	2–3	4–6	5–6	5–6
Industrial	8–10	7–9	7–8	7–8
Public and Semi-Public	6–8	6–8	10–12	10–12
Recreational	12–14	12–14	14–16	14–16
Transport and Communication	10–12	10–12	12–14	12–14
Agriculture, Water Bodies, and Special Areas	Remaining area	Remaining area	Remaining area	Remaining area
Total Developed Area	100	100	100	100

Source: Ministry of Urban Development (MOUD), Government of India. 2015. Urban and Regional Development Formulation and Implementation Guidelines (URDPFI) Volume I. https://mohua.gov.in/upload/uploadfiles/files/URDPFI%20Guidelines%20Vol%20I.pdf.

The city studies found that while some cities exceeded this share, others fell short of it. For example, the amount of land allotted to industrial development in Gangtok was 0.72% (114 ha) of the total planning area whereas Sonipat had allotted 22.38% (2,790 ha) of the total planning area. The nature of spatial allocations to industries will vary based on several factors including (i) the extent to which the cities depend on industrial development to bolster their local economies; (ii) the number of land-intensive industries and industrial units supported by the urban agglomeration; (iii) the presence of primary resources (raw materials) such as water bodies, mineral deposits, soil types, etc. impacting the feasibility of developing specific industry sectors; and (4) anthropogenic factors such as promotion of industrialization through policies and regulations, availability of technically trained labor, and a legacy of industrial development in the region.

Aligning Economic Vision and Investment Planning

City investment plans and master plans have to be worked out in tandem to realize their economic visions, ensure industrial growth, and improve people's overall quality of life.

Cities, their municipal corporations, and their urban development bodies should develop a capital investment plan, which provides a link between the municipality's strategic vision (ideally an economic vision as argued for earlier in this chapter), its urban land-use plan, and its annual budget. A best practice in municipal fiscal management is to prepare a multi-year capital improvement plan that identifies anticipated public infrastructure and investment projects, as well as a financing approach (World Bank n.d.). The method is gaining traction in India. For example, the Second Revised Draft Development Plan 2031 of Vadodara city includes formulating a city investment plan within the overall city development plan (VMD 2006 and VUDA 2007). The plan for Vadodara was structured as a 6-year scheduling of prioritized physical investments based on a gap analysis carried out by Vadodara Municipal Corporation. The plan's salient feature is the upgrading of services and infrastructure standards, which would help the city leverage and boost economic development. The investments aimed to ensure that the city reaches a minimum level of infrastructure services. Box 6.3 provides an example of interlinking spatial and economic planning and Box 6.4 describes an example of capital investment planning.

Box 6.3: Interlinking Spatial Planning with Economic Planning— The South African Case

South African urban spatial planning was reinvigorated by the introduction of the integrated development plan (IDP) process through the promulgation of the Local Government: Municipal Planning and Performance Management Regulations in 2001 (Laldaparsad et al. 2013). The IDP is an "idealistic and strategic" guideline for allocating resources and implementing state capital investments through the municipal budgetary process. It also functions as a guideline for regulating private investments. South African regulations also prescribe that a municipality's IDP must include a spatial development framework framed by broad guidelines. The municipal budget is the third component of this urban planning framework, and its most practical mechanism to implement spatial transformation (Laldaparsad et al. 2013).

The Johannesburg experience shows the critical importance of linking spatial planning, infrastructure, and budgets, as well as the importance of using good data and tools such as geographic information system-based decision-support systems. Linking spatial planning and infrastructure requires considerable engagement with stakeholders (in and outside of governing institutions) and an understanding of the politics associated with these processes (Todes 2012).

Sources: Laldaparsad, S., H. Geyer, H., and D. Plessis. 2013. The Reshaping of Urban Structure in South Africa through Municipal Capital Investment: Evidence from Three Municipalities. *Stads- En Streeksbeplanning*. 63: 37–48; Todes, A. 2012. New Directions in Spatial Planning? Linking Strategic Spatial Planning and Infrastructure Development. Journal of Planning Education and Research. 32(4): 400–14. https://doi.org/10.1177/0739456x12455665.

Box 6.4: Capital Investment Planning—City of Nis in Serbia

The Draft Capital Investment Plan of the City of Nis, Serbia is a strategically important document that defined the city's midterm development guidelines (for 2010–2015). The idea behind the plan was to enable the city to better use its budget capacities, define priorities, prepare project documents in a timely manner, and improve access to external sources of finance (e.g., European Union pre-accession funds, ministries' funds and programs, and other donor funds). Indirectly, all stakeholders relevant to city development were included in the process because they were able to submit project requests. The stakeholders comprised city departments; public enterprises; public utilities; and education, science, research, healthcare, and social welfare institutions. A total of 33 projects were selected and ranked through this process, wherein the top priority projects were for utility infrastructure and general infrastructure (such as reconstructing and expanding a local airport and developing a parking garage, a central wastewater treatment system, a farmers' market, and three social housing projects).

Source: Kaganova, O. 2011. Guidebook on Capital Investment Planning for Local Governments (No. 13). World Bank. https://openknowledge.worldbank.org/bitstream/handle/10986/17394/656000NWP00PUB07B0UDS13CIP00PUBLIC0.pdf?sequence=1&isAllowed=y (pp. 51–7) (accessed January–March 2022).

Land-Use Classifications Aligned with Technological and Economic Changes

Land-use classifications must be dynamic and aligned with technological and economic changes. A comprehensive and detailed review of all production units within urban areas is needed to ensure that planning bodies understand the range and scope of contemporary industries before classifying and regulating them.

If a master plan's definition of "industrial use" does not recognize emerging industrial developments, they may be unregulated and thus not get the support they need. Therefore, two changes are needed. First, the definition of "industrial use" must be considered dynamic, with the classification of industrial use land reviewed every 5 years or as needed. The second challenge pertains to inordinate approval delays that increase transaction costs. Lack of coordination between groups that assess projects and grant them permits increases the time taken to gain approvals and transaction costs. Many cities have adopted online building permission systems; however, firms need many other approvals. The solution is a single-window portal for scrutinizing and accepting industry projects. Cities such as Warangal have adopted this approach; other cities could consider following suit and learning from international good practices (an example is the automatic approval processes adopted in cities such as Singapore).

Time Horizons of Master Plans

A master plan's targeted planning period needs to be flexible. It should allow for actionable short-term milestones guided by long-term strategic visions preferably detailed in separate but nested documents.

Master plans are made for long periods, typically about 20 years, because they take a long-haul approach. A long-term perspective is essential, but it needs to be flexible in the face of change. Pioneering cities such as Tokyo have addressed these challenges. Tokyo retained the master planning model of urban development by organizing the National Capital Region (NCR) Development Plan into three components: "essential" (with a time horizon of approximately 10 years), "development" (about 5 years), and "annual" (every fiscal year) plans. The NCR Basic Plan included simple directions for developments in population size and land use while the NCR Development Plan set out the foundation for developing facilities such as roads and railways (RIUED 2019).

In India, master plans or development plans are created under the state town and country planning acts. In Gujarat, there is provision for revising the development plan in 10 years along with fresh surveys, if necessary.

Cluster-Based Planning and Creation of Technopoles

Cluster-based planning. Many industrial development projects require simultaneous, large-scale investments and business services for the investing firms to become profitable. Given the high fixed costs, not all of these requirements can be provided by the private sector. Cluster development is aimed at overcoming this problem by focusing on developing a specific sector in a designated area. The narrowest version of cluster development is an industrial park, which accommodates enterprises linked together in a specific sector. An industrial park is a planned site that is developed and managed to promote industrial development. Unlike areas where firms naturally locate to be close to suppliers and markets, industrial parks require deliberate effort: feasibility studies, master planning, construction, and follow-up management (Kim 2015).

The Korean experience offers relevant lessons. Three distinct phases of industrial policy marked the period of high industrialization in the Republic of Korea from the 1960s to the 1980s. In the 1960s, the main policy concern was promoting labor-intensive export industries and basic industrial production.

In the 1970s, the government aggressively pursued a selective industrial policy.[77] In the 1980s, it moved away from an active industrial policy toward industrial rationalization and innovation. Industrial policy of the Republic of Korea later focused on restoring balanced development by promoting small and medium-sized industries and regional economic activities. The change in industrial policy was accompanied by a shift in industrial location policy.[78] The large industrial complexes that emerged during the heavy and chemical industry drive were based on the cluster concept. Although the term "cluster" was not explicitly mentioned, it came into wide use in the policy arena of the Republic of Korea in the late 1990s as the government paid more attention to promoting regional industries (Kim 2015).

In summary, policymakers will have to manage lands more effectively to enable industrial and economic development. Sector-specific cluster development is one way to enable the industrial ecosystem. The sectors should be decided based on factors including local labor competencies, abundance of specific material resources, and lack of regional competition for the same industry. Cluster development is suggested as opposed to heavily debt-driven, separate one-off industrial park developments in different parts of the city and beyond. Indeed, the quick and compounding economic returns generated due to the narrowing of sectoral focus during the formation of initial industrial clusters in smaller cities and towns (such as Sivakasi, a fireworks manufacturing hub, and Morbi, a ceramics manufacturing hub) presents a pattern of industrialization that may be especially relevant for cities that do not yet have significant industrial legacies (such as Nalgonda and Navsari).

Creating technopoles. The contemporary wave of creating technopoles—a cluster of high-technology enterprises—in India features a hybridized model of industrial development, wherein the state takes responsibility for the use of primary resources while engaging private sector entities to develop and maintain the infrastructure and services required for integrated urban industrial clusters (Box 6.5).

An example is the Mahindra World City, Chennai—India's first integrated business city and corporate India's first operational special economic zone (SEZ). Mahindra World City was established in 2002 and is promoted by the Mahindra Group (a privately-owned Indian multinational conglomerate) in partnership with the state government's Tamil Nadu Industrial Development Corporation.[79] The development spans more than 607 ha (1,500 acres), comprising multisector SEZs and a domestic tariff area and houses more than 67 blue chip companies (such as BMW, B. Braun, Capgemini, and Infosys). Other complementary land uses at Mahindra World City include housing, a school, a multi-specialty hospital, a business hotel, a hostel for single working professionals, a commercial center, a sports and leisure club, and a post office.[80]

---

[77] "As the high growth of exports of consumer goods rapidly increased the demand for intermediate and capital goods, the government [of the Republic of Korea] passed a series of laws to institutionalize the promotion of selected industries including machinery (1967), shipbuilding (1967), textiles (1967), electronics (1969), petrochemicals (1970), steel (1970), and nonferrous metal smelting (1971)" (Kim 2015: 12).

[78] The industrial location policy of the Government of the Republic of Korea developed through various phases (such as industrial parks for exporting industries, large-scale industrial complexes, rural and regional industrial parks, and specialized regional clusters) over the decades as per the policy regimes and market feedback (Kim 2015).

[79] Tamil Nadu Industrial Corporation Ltd. https://tidco.com/ (accessed January–March 2022).

[80] Mahindra World City Chennai. https://www.mahindraworldcity.com/chennai/ (accessed January–March 2022).

Box 6.5: Developing Technopoles in India

A "technopole," or a high-technology cluster, is a center of high-tech manufacturing and information-based quaternary industry (Artz and Kamalipour 2003). Technopoles can be worldwide regions dedicated to technological innovation, as well as centers of rapid economic and technological growth as a result of agglomeration effects (Moretti 2012). The components of a technopole usually comprise local firms, universities, financial institutions, and public research organizations (Caves 2004). In India, as early as 2000, two cities (Bangalore and Hyderabad) were identified as potential technopoles, with special emphasis on the International Tech Park Ltd., Bangalore and Electronic City areas, and the Hyderabad Information Technology and Engineering Consultancy City region (Zand 2000).

A checklist for recreating Silicon Valley—referred to in Karnataka's 2000s-era information technology (IT) policy, inspired by NASSCOM-McKinsey findings—could have the following components: (i) anchor companies, (ii) research centers, (iii) universities, and (iv) venture capital. Such components are essential to founding a new technopole (Zand 2000). Technopoles in Germany include the IT cluster Rhine–Main–Neckar, the largest IT cluster in Europe (Wikipedia Contributors 2021). In Japan, technopoles were planned and developed by the Ministry of International Trade and Industry (Simmie 1994). Academia–industry linkages are one of the most important dynamics for establishing technopoles. For example, Frederick Terman, a professor at Stanford University, is credited with initiating many research and development initiatives in Silicon Valley, investing in start-ups, and even helping to establish the Stanford Industrial Park (Quan-Haase 2012).

Bangalore's standing as India's Silicon Valley is often attributed to public sector research and development institutions such as Hindustan Aeronautics Limited, the Indian Space Research Organisation, and the National Aeronautical Laboratories being based in the city. That the country's premier technical institute (the Indian Institute of Science) is in the city is also a factor as it provides locally accessible talent. This, combined with the state's aggressive tax rebate regime and preferential provision of services and utilities to newly established industries (Zand 2000), contributed to an academia–labor–policy nexus needed for a competitive modern technopole.

NASSCOM = National Association of Software and Services Companies.
Sources: Artz, L., and Y. Kamalipour, eds. 2003. *The Globalization of Corporate Media Hegemony*. State University of New York Press; Caves, R. 2004. *Encyclopedia of the City*. Routledge; Moretti, E. 2012. *The New Geography of Jobs*. Houghton Mifflin Harcourt; Quan-Haase, A. 2012. *Technology and Society: Social Networks, Power, and Inequality*. Don Mills, Oxford University Press; Simmie, J. 1994. Technopole Planning in Britain, France, Japan and the USA. *Planning Practice & Research*; Wikipedia Contributors (2021); Technopole: https://en.wikipedia.org/wiki/Technopole; Zand, R. 2000. Technopoles of India? http://www.robzand.com/media/technopoles.pdf (accessed February 2022)..

The success of this approach is evidenced by it being used in Jaipur as the Mahindra World City—a 74:26 public–private partnership between the Mahindra Group and the Rajasthan State Industrial Development and Investment Corporation Ltd. The development is spread across about 1,214 ha (3,000 acres), with a multi-product SEZ on 607 ha (1,500 acres) and a domestic tariff area on 404 ha (1,000 acres).[81]

Such approaches are appropriate for cities in the post-industrial phase (such as Vadodara and Warangal) because they can leverage their proximity to competitive industrial clusters (Surat and Hyderabad, respectively) with an intensification of their strong academic base (colleges and other institutions) to achieve compounding effects in specific subsectors.[82]

---

[81] Mahindra World City Jaipur. https://www.mahindraworldcity.com/jaipur/ (accessed January–March 2022).
[82] Based on stakeholder consultations held by the study team up to December 2021 at Vadodara and Warangal.

Action Plan

The following recommendations are applicable to all cities.

(i) Adopt an integrative regional approach to planning by demarcating the larger urban region (the natural city) and planning city and commuting regions together.

(ii) Coordinate between agencies and align details in technical documents and implementation guidelines to integrate economic vision with master planning.

(iii) Develop annual action plans and nominate relevant implementing agencies.

(iv) Develop a capital investment plan to identify projects and schemes that are economically self-sustaining (preferably revenue-generating).

(v) Ensure that the master planning process and proposals allow for actionable short-term milestones guided by long-term strategic visions, preferably detailed in separate but nested documents. Timely revisions of the master plan are critical to ensure the document stays relevant.

(vi) Create statutory provisions enabling change in land-use definitions and regulations at predefined time periods. Make a comprehensive and detailed review of all production units within urban areas to ensure that planning bodies understand the range and scope of contemporary industries before classifying and regulating them.

(vii) Prepare project action plans for key proposals with milestones, relevant agencies, and their collaboration mechanisms.

(viii) Empower ULBs and metropolitan planning committees to undertake their mandates.

(ix) Develop cluster-based planning mechanisms and create technopoles based on local labor competencies, material resources, and connectivity through assistive and preferential policies.

Institutional Integration and Capacity Building in Development and Planning

The solutions for any specific city need to be adapted to institutional features at the state level and city-specific characteristics such as its size, the maturity of its institutional structures, and the extent of economic and industrial development. Some of the solutions are discussed here.

Remedy disjunctions between urban planning and economic visioning. Lack of coordination between agencies tasked with urban planning and economic visioning has resulted in a neglect of industrial/economic areas or zones within urban regions and/or the inability of the broader city–region to benefit from such zones through "spillover" benefits. One strategy to achieve coordination between urban planning and economic visioning is by including the ULBs and relevant urban departments in the economic planning and visioning processes—for example, through legal frameworks such as the Industrial Area Local Authority or Special Investment Region Acts. This should enable economic strategies to consider urban governance norms that can facilitate and sustain economic growth. Further, multiple timeframes need to be built into economic strategies (e.g., 5-, 10-, 20-, and 50-year periods) and appropriate governance actors and processes need to be identified for each period. This requires mechanisms that include relevant urban development departments, ministries, planning authorities, *panchayats* (village councils), and municipal corporations from the inception of economic planning through its execution, monitoring, and revision.

Solve overlapping functions or responsibilities. Review the diverse functions that local- and state-level agencies perform with the aim of rationalizing their roles and responsibilities. The resulting rationalization should help minimize overlaps and improve clarity and accountability. As urban regions grow and expand, governance boundaries should be revised periodically to reflect the realities.

Improve coordination and communication between stakeholders and institutions. Develop structures to streamline functions, institutions, and agencies and improve communication and coordination among the stakeholders, building on the review of functions to reduce overlapping roles and responsibilities.

Consider the promising models (and elements of such models) for resolving issues of overlapping functions and responsibilities and improving coordination between stakeholders and institutions. Such models include the NICDC SPV model that involves all stakeholders in the governance and administrative structure of industrial nodes by involving government, academia, and industry to promote the environment needed for technology start-ups and entrepreneurships.

Manage the lack of trained personnel in ULBs by investing directly in the expanding ULB staff to keep up with the demands that urban expansion places on local government. One way of enhancing ULBs' capacity to handle the increased demand is by developing a dedicated municipal cadre and lateral hiring of appropriately qualified individuals.

Programs that focus on building capacity and regularly upgrading knowledge and skills for ULBs need to be introduced and expanded. The trained personnel and the institutions involved in developing sustainable long-term economic growth must be equipped with tools, systems, and processes adequate to conduct their roles meaningfully over time. State governments could identify regional academic/research institutions that can deliver capacity building programs for their staff on a regular basis.

Several global agencies provide training for ULBs on the best practices adopted by various countries and their customizations for application in specific cases. For example, the Singapore Cooperation Enterprise is dedicated to supporting learnings from Singapore's successful economic and urban development and administration practices (Box 6.6). Partnerships with such agencies can be explored to ensure that the successful practices in urban and economic development can be adopted in Indian cities.

Box 6.6: Singapore Cooperation Enterprise

The Singapore Cooperation Enterprise (SCE) was set up by the Ministry of Trade and Industry and the Ministry of Foreign Affairs of Singapore in 2006 to respond effectively to the many foreign requests interested in Singapore's development experience. The SCE works closely with Singapore's 16 ministries and over 60 statutory boards to determine and tailor solutions that might match the needs of other governments and help meet their development objectives. The SCE also serves as the focal point for Singapore's public agencies to access such expertise. The SCE has partnered and collaborated with various states on urban development and governance areas, and has collaborated with NITI Aayog on urban planning, wastewater management, solid waste management, and public financing.

Source: Singapore Cooperation Enterprise. About Us. https://sce.org.sg/about-us.aspx.

Empower urban management bodies. ULBs must be empowered to enable cities and towns to effectively envision, plan, and implement their infrastructure and services, and to strengthen the governance structure and help implement larger visions and plans. Competent and mature urban management is necessary for successful industrial and city growth. While access to technical and analytical consultancy can be outsourced, empowering the overseeing bodies themselves requires a paradigm shift. The examples pioneered by Tokyo city (where an elected metropolitan assembly makes all decisions for the metropolitan region of Tokyo) and the Verband Region model (e.g., Stuttgart, Germany) are cases in point.[83]

An Indian equivalent for such an urban management model is the metropolitan planning committee, as mandated by the Constitution of India. A metropolitan area is defined as having at least 1 million people. Article 243ZE of the 74th Amendment to the Constitution notes: "There shall be constituted in every Metropolitan area, a Metropolitan Planning Committee to prepare a draft development plan for the Metropolitan Region as a whole."[84]

Policies and Regulations Governing Business Activity in Cities

To attract investment, a city needs to play a large role in promoting investments in its jurisdiction and to work with relevant state and central government agencies to create a simple regulatory approval process for businesses investing in the city. For context, it is useful to consider the experiences of a few cities in and beyond India. Table 6.3 describes briefly how some cities have structured their business-related policies and regulations, mainly focused on activities related to investment promotion and initiatives to streamline regulatory processes. The last column of Table 6.3 highlights some pertinent features of efforts to attract investments and spur economic activity, especially in services—which are generally overlooked in state industrial policies (which tend to focus on manufacturing).

---

[83] For Tokyo: Tokyo Gikai. (n.d.). Functions of the Metropolitan Assembly. Tokyo Metropolitan Gikai. https://www.gikai.metro.tokyo.jp/english/functions.html (accessed Q1 2022) and for Stuttgart: Stuttgart, V. R. (n.d.). Verband Region Stuttgart: Politics & Administration. Verband Region Stuttgart. https://www.region-stuttgart.org/andere-laender/english/politics-administration/?noMobile=1 (accessed Q1 2022).

[84] CivicSpace.in. 2009. Study on Setting up a Metropolitan Planning Committee for Bangalore 20.09.09. https://civicspace.in/wp-content/uploads/2019/10/Study-on-Setting-up-a-Metropolitan-Planning-Committee-for-Bangalore-20.09.09-1-f-1.pdf (p. 1) (accessed Q1 2022).

Table 6.3: Examples of Policies and Regulations at the City Level

City/ Country	Study Area	Selected Features
Dubai, United Arab Emirates[a]	Investment promotion	Dubai FDI is a dedicated agency under the Government of Dubai. The agency provides essential information and support to foreign businesses considering investing in Dubai's thriving economy and taking advantage of its global strategic importance. Among others, Dubai FDI provides support for obtaining regulatory approvals and liaising with public agencies/ authorities.
Stockholm, Sweden[b]	Investment promotion	Invest Stockholm is Stockholm's official investment promotion agency and is tasked with marketing and developing the Stockholm region as a business destination. The agency is owned by the city of Stockholm and promotes investments in the city across all the key sectors with a focus on innovation, upcoming sectors, and startups. The agency has partnerships with institutions spanning all areas relevant to business decisions on entry and/or expansion, including ■ accounting, ■ audit, ■ banks, ■ corporate mobility and work permits, ■ events, ■ insurance, ■ law firms, ■ property owners and real estate consultants, ■ pension providers, ■ public relations and influencer agencies, and ■ recruitment. All the services provided by Invest Stockholm are specific to the needs of investors and are provided free of charge.
Bilbao, Spain[c]	Investment promotion	The Bilbao City Council is mandated to drive and handle economic development of the city by aligning all stakeholders, government entities, and private sector actors that are involved in approval processes and for executing strategic projects.
Zurich, Switzerland[d]	Regulatory support, ease of doing business	Greater Zurich Area Ltd. (the official investment promotion agency of the economic region of Zurich) provides integrated and digitalized services through a single platform, enhancing service through faster turnaround times and easy dissemination of information. A dedicated technology services department and platform eases the handling of knowledge management, content management, return of investment, and synchronization with multiple departments.
New Delhi, India[e]	Regulatory support, ease of doing business	The Government of New Delhi has launched a new single window portal for the hospitality industry. This portal (which has simplified navigation and an easy-to-fill form) enables businesses, enterprises, and business personnel to get and renew licenses from five different agencies simultaneously within 49 days. The agencies include the Delhi Police, Municipal Corporation of Delhi, New Delhi Municipal Committee, Delhi Fire Service, and Delhi Pollution Control Committee. This is an important initiative as all the agencies have different jurisdictions and come under different levels of governments (i.e., central and state and city-level urban local bodies).

Sources:
[a] Dubai FDI. https://dubaifdi.gov.ae/page/en/about_dubai_fdi.
[b] Invest Stockholm. https://www.stockholmbusinessregion.com/who-we-are/.
[c] Bilbao. OECD Regional Development Papers (CFE/RDPC/URB(2022)4); Inclusive Growth and Resilience in Bilbao, Spain.
[d] Greater Zurich Area Ltd. https://www.greaterzuricharea.com/en/about-us-gza.
[e] New Delhi Single Window Portal. https://www.cnbctv18.com/business/delhi-licence-single-window-portal-eateries-lodging-establishments-lieutenant-governor-16060081.htm.

Recommendations

The key takeaway for this study's cities and others in India is that to attract investments and position a city as a destination for investors, attention needs to be paid to policies used to attract and showcase investment opportunities in the city and to regulations that provide a business climate favorable for investment, particularly in service industries.

Regarding policies for promoting investments in a city, marketing efforts should be aligned to the economic vision that has been developed for the city.[85] This entails creating a plan to identify an outreach medium to prospective investors, among others. A related initiative (which may be relevant for large cities or for city-regions) is the formulation of an investment promotion agency at the city level. Which arm of the government such an agency is housed with and how it coordinates with relevant agencies and stakeholders needs to be worked out by individual states.

A more challenging element of policies concerns whether cities should offer specific fiscal or nonfiscal incentives for attracting investments. Given the governance structure of India's cities, these issues need to be taken up by relevant state agencies (for example, the industry department, for attracting investments in manufacturing, and other state agencies, for services such as education, finance, hospitality, and retail). Further, how effective the incentives are should be given careful consideration—a complex and complicated topic.[86]

Less controversial are interventions aimed at improving a city's business climate by streamlining business regulations. Four areas are important:

(i) **Provide simple approval processes to enhance the ease of doing business.** Adopt a simplified framework of approval processes for setting up a business to reduce the time required for approvals from multiple authorities.

(ii) **Create a city-level single window for service industries.** Collaborate with the state and the central government and create a single window system that combines all the permissions required at the city, state, and central level for setting up and operating businesses in the city and for facilitating renewals of permissions.

(iii) **Empower local bodies in and for industrial areas not under ULBs.** This is to better coordinate the functions and activities of industry and urban development departments.

(iv) **Enact legislation mandating time-bound services.** Enable an automated/digital approval mechanism (to be recognized by all state and ULB departments) to mandate time-bound services provision in the city.[87]

---

[85] The issue of whether cities should offer fiscal and nonfiscal incentives is beyond the scope of this study.
[86] When the technology and e-commerce company Amazon announced in 2017 plans to build a second headquarters in North America, for example, more than 200 cities in Canada, Mexico, and the United States placed bids. There is no simple answer to the pay-off of such endeavors (known as "place-based policies" in the academic literature). However, some efforts, especially those aligned with a city's comparative advantage, are likely to be more effective than others and may be worthwhile.
[87] Such a system has been enacted in the new single window system for the hospitality industries in the National Capital Region and enables getting and renewing licenses from five agencies simultaneously within a fixed timeframe of 49 days.

References

Artz, L., and Y. Kamalipour, eds. 2003. *The Globalization of Corporate Media Hegemony*. State University of New York Press.

Caves, R. 2004. *Encyclopedia of the City*. Routledge. p. 662.

CivicSpace.in. 2009. Study on Setting up a Metropolitan Planning Committee for Bangalore 20.09.09. https://civicspace.in/wp-content/uploads/2019/10/Study-on-Setting-up-a-Metropolitan-Planning-Committee-for-Bangalore-20.09.09-1-f-1.pdf (p. 1) (accessed January–March 2022).

Commissioner and Director of Municipal Administration, Government of Andhra Pradesh. https://cdma.ap.gov.in/node/222#:~:text=Machilipatnam%20municipality%20has%20an%20area,km%20with%2042%20revenue%20wards (accessed 17 July 2022).

Dalal, S. 2008. Satish Magar Narrates to *MoneyLIFE* How He Created Magarpatta. *MoneyLIFE*. Mumbai, Moneywise Media Pvt. Ltd. https://www.moneylife.in/article/our-township-has-acted-as-an-agent-of-social-change-through-a-policy-of-inclusion-satish-magar/1304.html (accessed February 2022).

Deshmukh, P. 2008. Interview in Pune, India. 2008.

Deuskar, C. 2011. *A Better Way to Grow? Land Readjustment through Town Planning Schemes in Ahmedabad*. (Doctoral dissertation, Massachusetts Institute of Technology).

Ganguli, R. 2008. The Magarpatta Model for Land Acquisition. *Info Change News and Features*. http://infochangeindia.org/agenda/battles-overland/the-magarpatta-model-for-landacquisition.html (accessed February 2022).

Government of Gujarat. 2009. The Gujarat Special Investment Region Act, 2009. *The Gujarat Government Gazette*. Gujarat. https://gidc.gujarat.gov.in/pdf/act-and-rules/SIR_ACT_new.pdf p. 1.

Government of India, Ministry of Finance. Union Budget 2023. https://www.indiabudget.gov.in/.

Government of Madhya Pradesh. 2022. Contribution of Madhya Pradesh in National Goal of $5 Trillion Economy. Madhya Pradesh State Policy and Planning Commission. http://mpplanningcommission.gov.in/CONTRIBTION.pdf.

Grover, A., S. Lall, and W. Maloney. 2022. *Place, Productivity, and Prosperity: Revisiting Spatially Targeted Policies for Regional Development*. World Bank. doi:10.1596/978-1-4648-1670-3. License: Creative Commons Attribution CC BY 3.0 IGO

Infrastructure Development Finance Company (IDFC). 2010. Land Pooling and Reconstitution: A Self-Financing Mechanism for Urban Development. *Policy Group Quarterly*. No. 7

International Labour Organization (ILO). 2014. *Boosting Local Economies*. Part of Sustainable Enterprise Programme. International Labour Organization.

Kaganova, O. 2011. *Guidebook on Capital Investment Planning for Local Governments* (No. 13). World Bank. https://openknowledge.worldbank.org/bitstream/handle/10986/17394/656000NWP00PUB07B0UDS13CIP00PUBLIC0.pdf?sequence=1&isAllowed=y (pp. 51–7) (accessed January–March 2022).

Kim, Jong-il. 2015. *Lessons for South Asia from the Industrial Cluster Development Experience of the Republic of Korea*. Asia Development Bank. p. 9. https://www.adb.org/sites/default/files/publication/173136/south-asia-wp-037.pdf.

Laldaparsad, S., H. Geyer, H., and D. Plessis. 2013. The Reshaping of Urban Structure in South Africa through Municipal Capital Investment: Evidence from Three Municipalities. *Stads- En Streeksbeplanning*. 63: 37–48.

Leff, S., and B. Petersen. 2015. *Beyond the Scorecard: Understanding Global City Rankings.* The Chicago Council on Global Affairs. https://globalaffairs.org/research/report/beyond-scorecard-understanding-global-city-rankings.

Machilipatnam Urban Development Authority. https://krishna.ap.gov.in/machilipatnam-urban-development-authority-muda/ (accessed 17 July 2022).

Mahindra World City Chennai. https://www.mahindraworldcity.com/chennai/ (accessed January–March 2022).

Mahindra World City Jaipur. https://www.mahindraworldcity.com/jaipur/ (accessed January–March 2022).

Mathews, R., A. Kundu, P. Chawla, R. Palanichamy, M. Pai, and T. Sebastian. Forthcoming. *Evolution and Morphology of Delhi- National Capital Region's Economic Geography and Implications for Planning.* World Resources Institute.

Ministry of Urban Development (MOUD), Government of India. 2015. *Urban and Regional Development Formulation and Implementation Guidelines (URDPFI) Volume I.* https://mohua.gov.in/upload/uploadfiles/files/URDPFI%20Guidelines%20Vol%20I.pdf.

Moretti, E. 2012. *The New Geography of Jobs.* Houghton Mifflin Harcourt.

Moseley, M. 1974. Growth Centres in Spatial Planning (1st ed.). Pergamon. pp. 39-40.

National Industrial Corridor Development Programme (NICDC). https://www.nicdc.in/

New York City (NYC). 2022. *Rebuild, Renew, Reinvent: A Blueprint for New York City's Economic Recovery.*

New York City Economic Development Corporation (NYC EDC) n.d. *NYC Difference.* Economic Development Corporation. https://edc.nyc/why-nyc#:~:text=With%20a%20gross%20metropolitan%20product,countries%20like%20Canada%20and%20Russia

NITI Aayog. 2018. *Strategy for New India@75.* Government of India.

———. 2021. Reforms in Urban Planning Capacity in India: Final Report. https://www.niti.gov.in/sites/default/files/2021-09/UrbanPlanningCapacity-in-India-16092021.pdf

Quan-Haase, A. 2012. *Technology and Society: Social Networks, Power, and Inequality.* Don Mills, Oxford University Press.

Research Institute of Urban and Environmental Development (RIUED). 2019. Case Study on Tokyo Metropolitan Region, Japan. World Bank. https://openknowledge.worldbank.org/handle/10986/31941?show=full (pp 14–15).

Sami, N. 2012. From Farming to Development: Urban Coalitions in Pune, India. International Journal of Urban and Regional Research (1): 151-164.

Sanyal, B. and C. Deuskar. 2012. Town Planning Schemes as a Hybrid Land Readjustment Process in Ahmedabad, India. *Value Capture and Land Policies. Cambridge MA: Lincoln Institute of Land Policy.* pp 149–82,

Simmie, J. 1994. Technopole Planning in Britain, France, Japan and the USA. *Planning Practice & Research.* 9(1).

Singapore Cooperation Enterprise. About Us. https://sce.org.sg/about-us.aspx.

Stuttgart, V. R. n.d. Verband Region Stuttgart: Politics & Administration. Verband Region Stuttgart. https://www.region-stuttgart.org/andere-laender/english/politics-administration/?noMobile=1 (accessed first quarter 2022).

Tamil Nadu Industrial Corporation Ltd. https://tidco.com/ (accessed first quarter 2022).

Technopole: https://en.wikipedia.org/wiki/Technopole.

Todes, A. 2012. New Directions in Spatial Planning? Linking Strategic Spatial Planning and Infrastructure Development. Journal of Planning Education and Research. 32(4): 400–14. https://doi.org/10.1177/0739456x12455665.

Tokyo Gikai. n.d. Functions of the Metropolitan Assembly. Tokyo Metropolitan Gikai. https://www.gikai.metro.tokyo.jp/english/functions.html (accessed first quarter 2022).

United Nations Human Settlements Programme (UN HABITAT). 2005. *Promoting Local Economic Development through Strategic Planning, Volume 1: Quick Guide.* United Nations Human Settlements Programme.

Vadodara Municipal Corporation (VMC). 2006. *Preparation of a City Investment Plan (CIP) and Financing Strategies.* https://vmc.gov.in/pdf/Link_9.pdf (accessed December 2021).

Vadodara Urban Development Authority (VUDA). 2007. Second Revised Draft Development Plan 2031 – Vadodara. VUDA. https://in.b-ok.as/book/11677566/b78dfc (accessed December 2021).

Wikipedia Contributors. 2021. Technopole. https://en.wikipedia.org/wiki/Technopole (accessed February 2022).

World Bank. n.d. Capital Investment Planning. https://urban-regeneration.worldbank.org/node/12 (accessed February 2022).

Zand, R. 2000. Technopoles of India? http://www.robzand.com/media/technopoles.pdf.

Chapter 7

Conclusions

Cities in India occupy only 3% of the nation's land, but they contribute about half or more of gross domestic product. Although hard data are difficult to come by, the underlying economic dynamism the cities' contribution represents is likely driven primarily by India's largest cities, with many other cities not meeting their potential as engines of economic growth and job creation. Further, congestion and a lack of metropolitan planning may be holding back even the largest cities from realizing their full economic potential.

Factors responsible for this include inadequate investment in urban infrastructure, fragmented responsibilities between and among state government agencies and urban local bodies (ULBs), and ULBs' limited ownership of economic initiatives.

To discover possible solutions for the issues, the study team consulted with government and private sector stakeholders across project states, cities, and other major urban centers in India. The consultations were aimed at understanding the broader economic–spatial relations, urban and peri-urban dynamics, and reality of doing business in a regional setting. Cities in India and overseas were also studied to derive relevant lessons.

Five areas for states and cities to consider are proposed in this study, pertaining to the needs for (i) integrated economic vision for cities, (ii) integrated master planning to enable the integration of land-use and infrastructure provision, (iii) land supply and regulations that enable economic development, (iv) capacity development and mechanisms for institutional integration, and (v) policies and regulations that promote investment.

This final chapter summarizes the study's proposed interventions for states and cities in India across the five areas. The current and envisaged initiatives planned by state and city agencies need to be carefully considered as to whether they align with the study's findings. This will be important for ensuring that India's cities deliver on the promise that urbanization holds.

To develop an economic vision

- institute a city economic council with a governance structure that is tailored to state and city characteristics;

- ensure that the council is supported by representatives from the private sector and experts in economic and urban development;

- ensure that the economic vision for the city has a regional spatial strategy aligned with it;
- create city partnerships for thematic development opportunities and implementation; and
- develop a graded and certified program for enhancing the capacity of key stakeholders involved in planning and implementing the economic vision.

To supply land needed for development

- modernize and digitize the land records systems and make them interoperable across departments;
- integrate institutions of revenue, registration, and survey at the state level to harmonize land records data;
- establish integrated digital technology platforms to improve the efficiency of land transactions; and
- explore participatory land assembly mechanisms.

To achieve integrated master planning aligned with economic goals

- adopt a regional approach to planning by (i) demarcating the larger urban region, and (ii) planning the city and commuting area together;
- ensure that the master plan allows for actionable short-term milestones guided by a long-term strategic vision;
- develop a capital investment plan to identify projects that are aligned with the city's economic vision, economically sound, and self-sustaining;
- explore developing a cluster-based planning mechanism based on local labor competencies, material resources, and connectivity considerations;
- create provisions that facilitate change in land-use definitions and regulations at predefined time periods and with a detailed understanding of the range and scope of contemporary industries;
- coordinate among agencies and align details in technical documents and implementation guidelines to integrate the economic vision with the master plan;
- formulate an interdepartmental team led by appropriate officials to check the progress and outcomes of projects; and
- prepare project action plans for key proposals, specifying milestones, relevant agencies, and their collaboration mechanisms.

To strengthen institutional frameworks and build capacity

- create mechanisms enabling ULBs and relevant urban departments to participate in economic planning and visioning processes;

- engage public and private stakeholders in integrated approaches that bring together urban planning and economic visioning processes across levels and sectors;

- build multiple timeframes into economic strategies (5-, 10-, and 20-year periods), and incorporate incentives for public agencies to identify and respond to the needs of local populations and communities;

- review the functions that local and state-level agencies perform and rationalize their roles and responsibilities to minimize overlaps and improve clarity and accountability;

- reduce overlapping roles and responsibilities by developing structures to streamline functions across levels and improve communication and coordination;

- invest directly in expanding ULB staff to keep up with the demands of urban expansion; and

- expand support and training programs focusing on building capacity and regularly upgrading knowledge and skills.

To create a policy and regulatory environment conducive to business activity

- develop city-specific marketing programs (aligned with the city's vision) to support investments in the city;

- explore setting up an investment promotion agency for cities;

- create city-level single window facilities for service industries based within city limits (such as hospitality, healthcare, commercial developments, and education);

- enable, more generally, automated/digital approval mechanisms that are recognized by all state and ULB departments and mandate timebound services provision for businesses in the city; and

- empower local bodies in and for industrial areas not under ULBs to better coordinate the functions and activities of industry and urban development departments.

www.ingramcontent.com/pod-product-compliance
Lightning Source LLC
Chambersburg PA
CBHW041247240426
43669CB00028B/3001